Lingua Latina A1
Latin – English
Interlinear Short Stories
on Roman Life

Brian Smith

Copyright 2024

Brian Smith

Servus in Roma

Capitulum I: Captura in Silva

In silvis Germaniae, Arminius, iuvenis bellator Germanicus, venatur. Solus est, sagittis suis confidens.

In the forests of Germany, Arminius, a young Germanic warrior, hunts. He is alone, confident in his arrows.

Subito, legionarii Romani appropinquant. Missionem habent, tribus indigenis subigendis. Arminius eos conspicit et se celat.

Suddenly, Roman legionaries approach. They have a mission to subdue the local tribes. Arminius sees them and hides himself.

"Ecce! Germanus illic!" exclamat Romanus. "Capite eum!"

"Look! A German over there!" exclaims a Roman. "Capture him!"

Arminius fugere conatur, sed circumdatus est. Pugna incipit. Gladio et scuto armatus, fortiter pugnat.

Arminius tries to flee, but he is surrounded. The battle begins. Armed with a sword and shield, he fights bravely.

"Pro libertate!" Arminius clamat, sed hostes plures sunt.

"For freedom!" Arminius shouts, but the enemies are too many.

Legionarii, armis superioribus instructi, Arminium superant. Gladio vulneratus cadit.

The legionaries, equipped with superior weapons, overpower Arminius. Wounded by a sword, he falls.

"Vincimus!" exclamat centurio Romanus. "Eum in captivitatem ducimus."

"We win!" the Roman centurion exclaims. "We will take him into captivity."

Arminius captus, vinculis ligatur. Circumstantes de eius tribu videntur fugere. Solus et captus relinquitur.

Captured, Arminius is bound with chains. The people from his tribe seem to flee. He is left alone and captured.

Dum Romani eum ducunt, Arminius cogitat de futuro suo incerto. Timet quid Romae accidat.

As the Romans lead him away, Arminius thinks about his uncertain future. He fears what will happen in Rome.

"Quid mihi fiet?" Arminius tacite interrogat.

"What will become of me?" Arminius silently asks.

Capitulum II: Iter ad Romam

Arminius, vinculis ligatus, cum custodibus Romanis iter Romam incipit. Multa milia passuum ante se habet.

Arminius, bound in chains, begins the journey to Rome with his Roman guards. He has many miles ahead of him.

Per viam, magnitudinem et diversitatem Imperii Romani videt. Homines varii, vestes diversas gerentes, circum eum sunt.

Along the way, he sees the vastness and diversity of the Roman Empire. Various people, wearing different clothes, are around him.

Cum aliis captivis ex diversis terris colloquitur. "Unde venis?" rogat captivus. "Ex Germania," Arminius respondet.

He speaks with other captives from different lands. "Where are you from?" asks a captive. "From Germany," Arminius replies.

Arminius linguam Latinam discere incipit. Simplices phrases ut "Salve!" et "Quid agis?" ei docentur.

Arminius begins to learn the Latin language. Simple phrases like "Hello!" and "How are you?" are taught to him.

Iter eum per varias urbes et colonias Romanas ducit. Arminius vias stratas, aquaeductus, et aedificia Romana observat.

The journey takes him through various Roman cities and colonies. Arminius observes paved roads, aqueducts, and Roman buildings.

Primum cibum Romanum gustat. "Hoc est panis et olivae," dicit custos. Arminius novos sapores experitur.

He tastes Roman food for the first time. "This is bread and olives," says a guard. Arminius experiences new flavors.

Noctes sub astris in castris Romanis agit. Arminius caelum spectat, stellas numerans.

He spends nights under the stars in Roman camps. Arminius watches the sky, counting the stars.

Milites Romani de captivis et itinere suo loquuntur. "Romae, hi servi erunt," unum audit dicentem.

The Roman soldiers talk about the captives and their journey. "In Rome, these will be slaves," he hears one say.

Arminius de libertate amissa et patria sua cogitat. "Numquamne Germaniam videbo?" secum putat.

Arminius thinks about his lost freedom and homeland. "Will I never see Germany again?" he wonders to himself.

Dies et noctes transeunt, et Roma appropinquat. Arminius sentit se ad novam vitam accedere.

Days and nights pass, and Rome draws near. Arminius feels himself approaching a new life.

Capitulum III: Prima Nox Romae

Tandem Romam perventum est. Arminius, vinculis liberatus, per magnas turbidasque urbis vias ducitur. Urbs magna et splendida est, sed etiam terribilis.

At last, Rome is reached. Arminius, freed from his chains, is led through the great and bustling streets of the city. The city is large and splendid, but also terrifying.

In viis, multa et varia videt: aedificia alta, populum frequentem, mercatores clamantes. Omnia nova et mira sunt.

In the streets, he sees many different things: tall buildings, crowded people, merchants shouting. Everything is new and strange.

Colosseum, amphitheatrum ingens, conspicit. "Quam magnum est!" inquit. Magnitudinem et potentiam Romae miratur.

He sees the Colosseum, a huge amphitheater. "How large it is!" he says. He marvels at the size and power of Rome.

In foro, ubi servi venduntur, Arminius stat. Venditor clamat: "Fortis Germanicus ad vendendum!" Multa ocula eum spectant.

In the forum, where slaves are sold, Arminius stands. The seller shouts: "A strong German for sale!" Many eyes are watching him.

In foro, nova verba discit: "pretium", "mercatus", "emere". Haec verba saepe audit.

In the forum, he learns new words: "price", "market", "to buy". He hears these words often.

Senator Romanus dives Arminum emere decernit. "Hic mihi serviet," inquit senator. Arminius novum dominum habet.

A wealthy Roman senator decides to buy Arminius. "He will serve me," the senator says. Arminius has a new master.

Dominum suum primum videt. "Ego sum tuus dominus," inquit ille. "In villa mea laborabis." Arminius timet et tacet.

He sees his master for the first time. "I am your master," he says. "You will work in my villa." Arminius is afraid and silent.

Arminius indumenta nova et locum ad dormiendum in villa senatoris accipit. Omnia aliena et diversa sunt.

Arminius receives new clothes and a place to sleep in the senator's villa. Everything is foreign and different.

Alios servos in domo senatoris convenit. "Salve," dicunt. "Nos servi sumus." Arminius salutat, sed anxius est.

He meets other slaves in the senator's house. "Hello," they say. "We are slaves." Arminius greets them, but he is anxious.

Nocte prima Romae, Arminius somnum capere non potest. Multa cogitat: libertatem, familiam, futurum incertum.

On his first night in Rome, Arminius cannot sleep. He thinks about many things: freedom, family, an uncertain future.

Capitulum IV: Domus Domini

*In villa Romana, Arminius vitam novam discit. Omnia in villa
sunt diversa ab eius vita priori.*

In the Roman villa, Arminius learns a new life. Everything in the
villa is different from his previous life.

*Arminius verba domestica Latina discit: "culina", "hortus",
"cubiculum". Haec verba cotidie utitur.*

Arminius learns household Latin words: "kitchen", "garden",
"bedroom". He uses these words every day.

*In hortis villae laborare iubetur. Plantas curat et aquam portat.
Labor est durus, sed Arminius cito discit.*

He is ordered to work in the villa's gardens. He tends the plants and carries water. The work is hard, but Arminius learns quickly.

Cum aliis servis ex diversis terris colloquitur. "Unde venis?" rogat. "Ego ex Aegypto," respondet servus.

He speaks with other slaves from different lands. "Where are you from?" he asks. "I am from Egypt," a slave replies.

Familiam Romanam observat. Pater familias severus est, mater et liberi in villa vivunt. Mores familiares Romanos discit.

He observes the Roman family. The father of the family is strict, and the mother and children live in the villa. He learns Roman family customs.

Interdum Arminius de domo sua et libertate perdita cogitat. Tristis est, sed laborare debet.

Sometimes Arminius thinks about his home and lost freedom. He is sad, but he must work.

De diis Romanis et ritibus religiosis audit. "Hodie sacrificium Iovi facimus," inquit alius servus.

He hears about the Roman gods and religious rites. "Today we make a sacrifice to Jupiter," says another slave.

Epulam magnam in villa participat. Cibum multum et bonum gustat. Romanorum epulae sunt copiosae.

He participates in a great feast in the villa. He tastes much and good food. Roman feasts are abundant.

Ordinem inter servos intellegit. Quosdam servos meliores esse videt, alios peiores. Hierarchia in villa est.

He understands the order among the slaves. He sees that some slaves are better, others worse. There is a hierarchy in the villa.

*Mores et voluntates domini discere incipit. "Dominus hoc amat,"
servus docet. "Hoc ei placet." Arminius observat et discit.*

He begins to learn the master's customs and desires. "The master
likes this," a slave teaches him. "This pleases him." Arminius
observes and learns.

Capitulum V: Forum Romanum

Arminius primum Forum Romanum visitat. Mandata a domino suo facere debet.

Arminius visits the Roman Forum for the first time. He must carry out orders from his master.

Forum plenum est et tumultuosum. Arminius mercatores, ementes, vendentesque videt. Aedificia publica magna et pulchra sunt.

The forum is crowded and chaotic. Arminius sees merchants, buyers, and sellers. The public buildings are large and beautiful.

In foro, verba nova discit: "emere", "vendere", "pretium". Haec verba in mercatu audit.

In the forum, he learns new words: "to buy", "to sell", "price". He hears these words in the market.

Orationem publicam a senatore Romano audit. Senator magnis verbis populum adloquitur. Arminius verba non omnia intellegit, sed oratoris potentiam sentit.

He hears a public speech by a Roman senator. The senator addresses the people with grand words. Arminius does not understand all the words, but he feels the orator's power.

Divites et pauperes in foro conspicit. "Cur tam magna differentia?" secum cogitat. Vestimenta et habitus diversi sunt.

He notices the rich and the poor in the forum. "Why is there such a great difference?" he thinks to himself. Their clothing and manners are different.

Iurgium legale in foro videt. Duo viri coram iudice contendunt. "De terra disputant," servus proximus explicat.

He sees a legal dispute in the forum. Two men are arguing before a judge. "They are disputing over land," explains a nearby slave.

De pecunia Romana et negotiis discit. "Haec est sestertius," servus docet. "In foro utimur."

He learns about Roman money and business. "This is a sestertius," a slave teaches him. "We use it in the forum."

Servum Germanicum invenit et cum eo loquitur. "Ego quoque ex Germania sum," inquit ille. "Salve, frater!" Arminius respondet.

He finds a German slave and speaks with him. "I am also from Germany," he says. "Hello, brother!" Arminius replies.

Processionem in honorem dei Romani videt. "Hodie festum est," dicit servus. "Deum celebramus." Processio est longa et sollemnis.

He sees a procession in honor of a Roman god. "Today is a festival," says a slave. "We are celebrating a god." The procession is long and solemn.

Ad villam redit, novam perspectivam vitae Romanae habens. Multa cogitat de foro, populo, et urbe.

He returns to the villa, having a new perspective on Roman life. He thinks much about the forum, the people, and the city.

Capitulum VI: Ludi et Spectacula

Arminius cum domino suo ad ludos Romanos in Colosseo vadit. Primum est sibi ludos spectare.

Arminius goes with his master to the Roman games in the Colosseum. It is his first time watching the games.

Gladiatores et pugnas ferarum videt. "Fortes et audaces sunt," inquit. Spectaculum excitans est, sed etiam crudele.

He sees gladiators and beast fights. "They are strong and bold," he says. The spectacle is exciting, but also cruel.

Verba ludi discit: "gladiator", "certamen", "victoria". Haec verba in Colosseo audit.

He learns the words of the games: "gladiator", "contest", "victory". He hears these words in the Colosseum.

Excitatio et saevitia ludorum eum afficiunt. Populus victoribus gladiatorum vehementer plaudit.

The excitement and brutality of the games affect him. The crowd cheers strongly for the victorious gladiators.

Cursus quadrigarum spectat. Multitudo plaudit et clamor tollitur. Energia multitudinis commovetur.

He watches the chariot races. The crowd applauds, and a great shout arises. He is moved by the energy of the crowd.

De otio et voluptatibus Romanorum discit. "Romani ludi spectaculaque amant," servus explicat.

He learns about Roman leisure and pleasures. "The Romans love games and spectacles," a slave explains.

Fabulam theatricam Latine videt. Histriones in scaena fabulam agunt. "Arte et voce mira sunt," Arminius cogitat.

He watches a theatrical play in Latin. Actors perform a play on stage. "Their skill and voices are remarkable," Arminius thinks.

Sentimenta de cultura Romana complexa habet. "Quam diversa est a cultura mea," secum putat.

He has complex feelings about Roman culture. "How different it is from my own culture," he thinks to himself.

Ad villam redit, eventus diei contemplans. "Roma miris plena est," inquit.

He returns to the villa, reflecting on the day's events. "Rome is full of wonders," he says.

Capitulum VII: Ars Romana

Arminius in convivio artificum Romanorum adiuvat. "Hodie multos artifices videbis," dominus ei dicit.

Arminius helps at a banquet of Roman artists. "Today you will see many artists," his master says to him.

Arminius verba artis discit: "statua", "mosaicum", "pictura". Haec verba inter artifices audit.

Arminius learns the words of art: "statue", "mosaic", "painting". He hears these words among the artists.

Sculpturas, mosaica, et picturas Romanas videt. "Quam pulchrae sunt!" inquit. Varitatem artis Romanae admiratur.

He sees Roman sculptures, mosaics, and paintings. "How beautiful they are!" he says. He admires the variety of Roman art.

Musicam et carmina Romana audit. Cantores et citharoedi in convivio sunt. "Musica Romanorum dulcis est," Arminius sentit.

He hears Roman music and songs. Singers and lyre players are at the banquet. "Roman music is sweet," Arminius feels.

Ars in societate Romana magni ponderis est. "Per artem culturam Romanam exprimimus," quidam artifex explicat.

Art is of great importance in Roman society. "Through art, we express Roman culture," one artist explains.

Ad epulam Romanam parandam adiuvat. "Hodie multa cibaria exquisita habebimus," coquus dicit. Arminius in culina laborat.

He helps prepare a Roman feast. "Today we will have many exquisite dishes," the cook says. Arminius works in the kitchen.

Cum civibus Romanis diversorum ordinum colloquitur. "Salve," dicunt. "Tu servus es?" Quidam amabiles sunt, alii superbi.

He talks with Roman citizens of different ranks. "Hello," they say. "Are you a slave?" Some are kind, others are arrogant.

De litteratura Romanorum et scriptoribus famosis discit. "Hic est liber Vergilii," quidam hospes ostendit. "Poeta clarus est."

He learns about Roman literature and famous writers. "This is a book by Vergil," a guest shows him. "He is a famous poet."

Aestimationem artis Romanae concipit. "Ars Romanorum mirabilis est," Arminius cogitat. "Illam magis magisque intellego."

He develops an appreciation for Roman art. "The art of the Romans is amazing," Arminius thinks. "I understand it more and more."

*Experientias Germanicas Romanasque miscet. "Germanus sum,
sed nunc etiam partem culturae Romanae agnosco," secum putat.*

He mixes his German and Roman experiences. "I am German, but
now I also recognize part of Roman culture," he thinks to himself.

Capitulum VIII: Amicitia et Amor

*Arminius cum aliis servis amicitias format. "Tu amicus meus es,"
saepe dicit. Inter servos communicatio augetur.*

Arminius forms friendships with the other slaves. "You are my
friend," he often says. Communication increases among the
slaves.

*Verba Latina sentimentorum et relationum discit: "amor",
"amicitia", "laetitia". Haec verba in colloquiis cotidianis utitur.*

He learns Latin words of feelings and relationships: "love",
"friendship", "joy". He uses these words in daily conversations.

*Cum Lydia, alia serva, familiarem se efficit. "Unde venis?"
Arminius eam interrogat. "Ego ex Graecia sum," Lydia
respondet.*

He becomes close with Lydia, another slave. "Where are you from?" Arminius asks her. "I am from Greece," Lydia replies.

De patriis suis et praeteritis fabulantur. Lydia de Graecia narrat, Arminius de Germania. "Interessant!" uterque dicit.

They talk about their homelands and pasts. Lydia talks about Greece, Arminius about Germany. "Fascinating!" they both say.

Arminius Lydiae verba Germanica docet. "Hoc 'salve' in lingua mea est," inquit. Lydia novis verbis gaudet.

Arminius teaches Lydia German words. "This is 'hello' in my language," he says. Lydia delights in the new words.

Nuptias Romanas spectat. "Quam pulchrae sunt!" inquit. Ritus et ceremonias Romanas observat.

He watches a Roman wedding. "How beautiful they are!" he says. He observes Roman rites and ceremonies.

De moribus coniugialibus Romanorum discit. "In matrimonio, vir et uxor coniunguntur," Lydia explicat. "Hoc foedus amoris est."

He learns about Roman marriage customs. "In marriage, husband and wife are joined," Lydia explains. "It is a bond of love."

Sentimenta mixta de suo statu in societate Romana habet. "Servus quidem sum, sed etiam pars huius mundi," secum cogitat.

He has mixed feelings about his status in Roman society. "I am indeed a slave, but I am also part of this world," he thinks to himself.

Celebrationem in honorem Veneris, deae amoris, adit. "Venus est dea amoris," Lydia dicit. Arminius festum et ritus Romanos spectat.

He attends a celebration in honor of Venus, the goddess of love. "Venus is the goddess of love," Lydia says. Arminius watches the festival and Roman rites.

Sensum pertinendi in terra aliena incipit habere. "Roma nunc mihi non tam aliena videtur," Arminius secum putat.

He begins to feel a sense of belonging in a foreign land. "Rome no longer seems so foreign to me," Arminius thinks to himself.

Capitulum IX: Conspiratio

Arminius insidias contra dominum suum audit. "Dominum nostrum interficere volunt," servus susurrat. Arminio hoc audito territur.

Arminius hears about a plot against his master. "They want to kill our master," a slave whispers. Arminius, having heard this, is terrified.

Conflictum inter fidelitatem erga dominum et societatem cum servis sentit. "Quid facere debeo?" secum cogitat.

He feels a conflict between loyalty to his master and solidarity with the slaves. "What should I do?" he thinks to himself.

Verba politica et iustitiae discit: "lex", "iustitia", "senatus". Haec verba in colloquiis audiuntur.

He learns political and justice-related words: "law", "justice", "senate". These words are heard in conversations.

Statuit dominum de insidiis monere. "Domine, periculum est," Arminius anxie dicit. Dominus audito Arminio statim agit.

He decides to warn his master about the plot. "Master, there is danger," Arminius says anxiously. Upon hearing Arminius, the master acts immediately.

Conspiratores comprehensi sunt, et Arminius pro fide laudatur. "Gratias tibi ago," dominus dicit. Arminius gratulationem accipit, sed de electione sua dubitat.

The conspirators are caught, and Arminius is praised for his loyalty. "Thank you," the master says. Arminius accepts the praise but doubts his decision.

Sentimenta contraria de decisione sua habet. "Recte feci?" se interrogat. "Amicosne meos prodidi?"

He has conflicting feelings about his decision. "Did I do the right thing?" he asks himself. "Did I betray my friends?"

Pro fidelitate sua, Arminius a domino suo maiorem libertatem in villa donatur. "Tibi confido," dominus dicit.

For his loyalty, Arminius is granted greater freedom in the villa by his master. "I trust you," the master says.

De lege et ordine Romano plura discit. "Romani legibus et ordine valde student," Lydia explicat.

He learns more about Roman law and order. "The Romans are very devoted to law and order," Lydia explains.

Respectum a servis aliis et quibusdam Romanis accipit. "Vir fidelis es," servus dicit. Arminius respectum sentit, sed etiam solitudinem.

He receives respect from other slaves and some Romans. "You are a loyal man," a slave says. Arminius feels respect, but also loneliness.

Complexitatem identitatis suae in societate Romana intellegit. "Ego Germanus sum, sed etiam pars huius mundi Romanorum," Arminius secum putat.

He understands the complexity of his identity in Roman society. "I am German, but I am also part of this Roman world," Arminius thinks to himself.

Capitulum X: Libertas

Dominus Arminium ad se vocat. "Pro fide tua, libertatem tibi do," inquit. Arminius liber factus est.

The master calls Arminius to him. "For your loyalty, I give you freedom," he says. Arminius has been made free.

Arminius inter manendum Romae et reditum in Germaniam dubitat. "Ubi est vera mea domus?" secum quaerit.

Arminius hesitates between staying in Rome and returning to Germany. "Where is my true home?" he asks himself.

De itinere suo et mutatione sua reflectit. "Multum mutatus sum," cogitat. "Roma me mutavit."

He reflects on his journey and his transformation. "I have changed a lot," he thinks. "Rome has changed me."

Verba libertatis et civitatis discit: "libertas", "civis", "iura". Haec verba nova sunt et grata.

He learns words of freedom and citizenship: "freedom", "citizen", "rights". These words are new and welcome to him.

Decernit Romae ut homo liber manere. "Roma nunc domus mea est," inquit. Sentit se ex Roma esse.

He decides to stay in Rome as a free man. "Rome is now my home," he says. He feels that he belongs to Rome.

Consilium capit ut hortulanus laboraret. "Hortos semper amavi," dicit. "Hoc facere volo."

He makes a decision to work as a gardener. "I have always loved gardens," he says. "This is what I want to do."

Desiderium habet hereditatem Germanicam suam in Roma colere. "Germanus quidem sum, sed etiam Romanus," secum putat.

He has a desire to honor his German heritage in Rome. "I am indeed German, but also Roman," he thinks to himself.

Culturas Romanam et Germanicam in identitate sua miscet. "Duo mundi in me vivunt," sentit.

He blends Roman and German cultures in his identity. "Two worlds live within me," he feels.

Spe futuri in societate Romana ut civis liber contribuere intendit. "Aliquid bonum facere possum," inquit.

With hope for the future, he intends to contribute as a free citizen in Roman society. "I can do something good," he says.

Fabula finitur cum spe et proposito novo Arminii Romae. "Ad futurum aspicio," Arminius dicit. "Roma et ego parati sumus."

The story ends with hope and Arminius' new purpose in Rome. "I look to the future," Arminius says. "Rome and I are ready."

In Britannia

Capitulum I: Iter ad Murum Hadriani

In urbe Roma, sub sole claro, Gaius, miles Romanus, per vias festinabat. Romam amabat – eius vias, fora, et maxime familiam suam. Sed hodie aliquid novi accidebat. Imperator eum ad Murum Hadriani, longe a Roma, mittere decreverat.

In the city of Rome, under the bright sun, Gaius, a Roman soldier, hurried through the streets. He loved Rome – its streets, forums, and especially his family. But today something new was happening. The Emperor had decided to send him to Hadrian's Wall, far from Rome.

Gaius, corde pleno amore et trepidatione, ad palatium Imperatoris venit. Imperator, vir gravis et potens, ante eum stetit. "Gaius," inquit Imperator, "Romae te esse necesse est. Ad septentriones i, Murum Hadriani custodi. Confido in te."

Gaius, with a heart full of love and apprehension, went to the Emperor's palace. The Emperor, a serious and powerful man, stood before him. "Gaius," the Emperor said, "Rome needs you. Go to the north, guard Hadrian's Wall. I trust in you."

Gaius, caput inclinans, respondit: "Imperatori meo et Romae semper fidelis ero. Ibo et muros nostros defendam."

Gaius, bowing his head, replied: "I will always be loyal to my Emperor and to Rome. I will go and defend our walls."

Itaque, cum legione sua, iter longum et difficile coepit. Per silvas densas et montes altos ibant, saepe de familiis et amicis suis cogitantes. Iter non solum corpora sed etiam animos militum probabat.

And so, with his legion, he began a long and difficult journey. They went through dense forests and high mountains, often thinking about their families and friends. The journey tested not only the soldiers' bodies but also their spirits.

Nocte una, in castris iuxta flumen, Gaius cum amicis suis sedebat. Caelum stellis plenum erat. "Scitisne," inquit Gaius, "me semper Romam in corde meo ferre? Familiam meam amo et nostrae urbis pulchritudinem."

One night, in a camp by a river, Gaius was sitting with his friends. The sky was full of stars. "Do you know," Gaius said, "that I always carry Rome in my heart? I love my family and the beauty of our city."

Amicus eius, Marcus nomine, risit et dixit: "Et ego, Gai. Sed scimus munere nostro magni momenti fungi. Murus Hadriani nos exspectat."

His friend, named Marcus, laughed and said: "And I too, Gaius. But we know our duty is of great importance. Hadrian's Wall awaits us."

Iter pergebant, die post die, interdum sub sole calido, interdum sub imbre frigido. Flumina transibant et montes superabant. Gaius saepe cogitabat de muris altis et frigidis quos mox aditurus erat.

They continued their journey, day after day, sometimes under the hot sun, sometimes in the cold rain. They crossed rivers and climbed mountains. Gaius often thought about the tall and cold walls he would soon reach.

Tandem, post multos dies, ad Murum Hadriani pervenerunt. Murus magnus et formidabilis in horizonte stetit, finis Romani imperii. Gaius, ad murum aspiciens, sentiebat se non solum Romae defensorem esse, sed etiam totius mundi Romani.

At last, after many days, they arrived at Hadrian's Wall. A great and formidable wall stood on the horizon, the edge of the Roman Empire. Gaius, looking at the wall, felt that he was not only a defender of Rome but of the entire Roman world.

"Ecce," inquit Gaius, "Murus Hadriani! Hic stamus pro Roma, pro familiis nostris, pro imperio nostro."

"Behold," said Gaius, "Hadrian's Wall! Here we stand for Rome, for our families, for our empire."

Militibus suis circumstantibus, Gaius sciebat multas aventuras ibi futuras se experiturum esse. Et cum prima stella in caelo nocte illa micuit, spem habuit se unum diem Romam, domum suam dulcem, reversurum esse.

With his soldiers standing around him, Gaius knew that many adventures awaited him there. And when the first star twinkled in the sky that night, he hoped that one day he would return to Rome, his sweet home.

Capitulum II: In Castris

Sub umbra Muri Hadriani, castra Romana posita erant. Gaius et alii milites tabernaculum commune dividebant. Nocturnus ventus murmurabat, et Gaius in strato suo iacebat, somnum captare conans.

Under the shadow of Hadrian's Wall, the Roman camp was set up. Gaius and the other soldiers shared a common tent. The night wind murmured, and Gaius lay on his bed, trying to catch sleep.

Prima luce, cornu sonuit. Omnes milites surrexerunt et ad exercitia militaria properaverunt. Gaius, armaturam suam induens, cogitabat de diebus in Roma. "Quam diversa est vita militaris," susurravit.

At first light, the horn sounded. All the soldiers rose and hurried to military exercises. Gaius, putting on his armor, thought about his days in Rome. "How different military life is," he whispered.

Exercitiis factis, Gaius et amici ad murum ambulaverunt. "Videtisne," inquit Gaius, "quantam responsabilitatem nostram esse? Hic, fines Romani imperii custodimus."

After the exercises were done, Gaius and his friends walked to the wall. "Do you see," said Gaius, "how great our responsibility is? Here, we guard the borders of the Roman Empire."

In castris, coquus cibum parabat. Gaius et amici ad ignem conveniebant, panem et carnes edentes. "Bene est hic esse," dixit Marcus, "sed etiam cibum Romae desidero."

In the camp, the cook was preparing food. Gaius and his friends gathered by the fire, eating bread and meat. "It's good to be here," said Marcus, "but I also miss the food in Rome."

Post cenam, centurio, vir severus et disciplinatus, milites ad se vocavit. "Audite!" exclamavit centurio. "Cras exercitia dura habebimus. Parati este!"

After dinner, the centurion, a strict and disciplined man, called the soldiers to him. "Listen!" the centurion exclaimed. "Tomorrow we will have hard exercises. Be prepared!"

Nocte illa, Gaius lucernam accendit et chartam cepit. Epistulam ad familiam suam scribere coepit. "Cara familia," scribebat, "hic in finibus mundi nostri sum. Vos desidero."

That night, Gaius lit a lamp and took some paper. He began to write a letter to his family. "Dear family," he wrote, "I am here on the borders of our world. I miss you."

Stilo posito, Gaius foras exiit. Ignis in medio castrorum ardebat, milites circum sedentes. Gaius ad caelum aspexit, stellas contemplans. "Forsitan," cogitavit, "eadem stellae super Romam nunc fulgent."

After setting down the pen, Gaius went outside. A fire burned in the middle of the camp, with soldiers sitting around it. Gaius looked up at the sky, contemplating the stars. "Perhaps," he thought, "these same stars are now shining over Rome."

Subito, tumultus ex uno angulo castrorum ortus est. Gaius et amici surrexerunt, gladios suos capientes. "Quid est?" clamavit Gaius.

Suddenly, a commotion arose from one corner of the camp. Gaius and his friends jumped up, grabbing their swords. "What is it?" shouted Gaius.

Erat falsus alarmus – animal silvestre in castra intraverat. Milites riserunt, animal recedente. "Videte," inquit Gaius ridens, "non solum barbari sunt qui nos terrere possunt."

It was a false alarm – a wild animal had entered the camp. The soldiers laughed as the animal retreated. "See," said Gaius, laughing, "it's not only barbarians who can scare us."

Nocte progrediente, Gaius ad stratum suum rediit. Cogitationes de Roma, familia, et vita futura eum tenebant. Sed sciebat munus suum in muro Hadriani magni momenti esse. Et cum primo lumine, novus dies in castris Romae incepit.

As the night progressed, Gaius returned to his bed. Thoughts of Rome, his family, and his future life occupied him. But he knew his duty on Hadrian's Wall was of great importance. And with the first light, a new day began in the Roman camp.

Capitulum III: Munus in Muro

In alto Muro Hadriani, Gaius vigilabat. Finitimos milites prope stantes vidit et eos amice salutavit. Ventus frigidus flabat, sed Gaius firmus et attentus stabat, arcum et sagittas portans.

On top of Hadrian's Wall, Gaius was keeping watch. He saw nearby soldiers standing close and greeted them warmly. A cold wind was blowing, but Gaius stood firm and alert, carrying his bow and arrows.

"Salve, Gai!" exclamavit Lucius, amicus eius. "Quid novi?"

"Hello, Gaius!" exclaimed Lucius, his friend. "What's new?"

Gaius respondit: "Nihil novi. Roma me desiderat."

Gaius responded: "Nothing new. I miss Rome."

Ambulabant in muro, de vita Romana fabulantes. Lucius de familia sua in urbe loquebatur, Gaius autem de campis et villis Romanis narrabat.

They walked on the wall, chatting about Roman life. Lucius spoke about his family in the city, but Gaius talked about the Roman fields and villas.

Subito, Gaius procul aliquid moveri vidit. "Videte!" inquit. "Forsitan barbari sunt!" Sed erant tantum animalia silvestria.

Suddenly, Gaius saw something move in the distance. "Look!" he said. "Maybe it's barbarians!" But it was just wild animals.

Cum sol occidere coepit, Gaius et Lucius ad castra redierunt. Frigus augebatur, et ventus validior fiebat. Gaius cibum ex pera sumpsit, panem et caseum edens.

As the sun began to set, Gaius and Lucius returned to the camp. The cold was increasing, and the wind was growing stronger. Gaius took food from his bag, eating bread and cheese.

"Roma," inquit Gaius, "ubi caelum semper serenum est, et venti non sunt tam frigidi."

"Rome," Gaius said, "where the sky is always clear, and the winds are not so cold."

Lucius risit. "Sed hic," respondit, "nos fortes et audaces esse debemus. Murus Hadriani nos custodit, et nos murum custodimus."

Lucius laughed. "But here," he replied, "we must be strong and brave. Hadrian's Wall protects us, and we protect the wall."

Sol iam occiderat, et tenebrae castra Romana tenebant. Gaius ad ignem sedebat, stellas contemplans. "Forsitan," cogitavit, "eadem stellae etiam super Romam nunc fulgent."

The sun had already set, and darkness covered the Roman camp. Gaius sat by the fire, contemplating the stars. "Perhaps," he thought, "the same stars are now shining over Rome."

Gaius, ad stratum suum rediens, de die futuro cogitabat. Munus in muro erat difficile, sed sciebat se et suos comites essentiales esse ad imperium Romanum defendendum. In somno, Roma in mente eius vivebat.

As Gaius returned to his bed, he thought about the coming day. The duty on the wall was difficult, but he knew that he and his comrades were essential to defending the Roman Empire. In his sleep, Rome lived in his mind.

Capitulum IV: In Vico Prope Murum

Gaius et amici eius, post diem longum et laboriosum, ad vicum prope Murum Hadriani ambulabant. Vesper erat, et caelum purpureum sole occidente fulgebat.

Gaius and his friends, after a long and laborious day, were walking to a village near Hadrian's Wall. It was evening, and the sky glowed purple as the sun set.

Ingressi sunt in cauponam, ubi lumen candelarum calidum et voces laetae eos exceperunt. "Hic, amici," inquit Gaius, "paulum relaxemus."

They entered an inn, where warm candlelight and cheerful voices greeted them. "Here, friends," said Gaius, "let's relax for a bit."

In caupona, vinum rubrum et suave biberunt. Gaius, calicem in manu tenens, dixit: "Pro salute nostra et Roma!"

In the inn, they drank smooth red wine. Gaius, holding his cup in hand, said: "For our health and for Rome!"

Conloquebantur cum incolis vicorum, de vita cotidiana et rebus simplicibus. Gaius de Roma et muro Hadriano narravit, incolae autem de vita ruris et familia. Risus et fabulae inter eos iucunde volabant.

They conversed with the villagers about daily life and simple matters. Gaius talked about Rome and Hadrian's Wall, while the villagers spoke about rural life and family. Laughter and stories pleasantly flew between them.

Mox, in lupanar intraverunt, ubi risus et musica erant. Gaius et amici sedebant, fabulas audientes et ridentes. "Hae sunt momenta quae vitam suavem faciunt," inquit Gaius.

Soon, they entered a tavern where laughter and music filled the air. Gaius and his friends sat, listening to stories and laughing. "These are the moments that make life sweet," said Gaius.

Cenam bonam edebant: panem, caseum, et carnes. Gaius, cibum gustans, dixit: "Nihil est melius quam cena bona cum amicis."

They ate a good meal: bread, cheese, and meat. Gaius, tasting the food, said: "Nothing is better than a good dinner with friends."

Musica in caupona erat, citharae sonos et tibiae melodiam faciebant. Omnes ad musicam movebantur, et quidam etiam saltare coeperunt.

There was music in the inn, with the sounds of lyres and the melody of flutes. Everyone was moving to the music, and some even began to dance.

Nox procedebat, et Gaius cum suis amicis sero in castra revertebatur. Via sub stellis erat tranquilla et pulchra.

The night went on, and Gaius, along with his friends, returned late to the camp. The road under the stars was peaceful and beautiful.

Dum ambulabant, Gaius de vita extra murum cogitabat. "Vita hic," inquit, "est diversa a vita in muro. Sed ubique munera nostra sunt."

As they walked, Gaius thought about life beyond the wall. "Life here," he said, "is different from life on the wall. But our duties are everywhere."

Cum ad castra pervenirent, omnes in lectos suos ceciderunt, fessi sed contenti. Gaius, ante somnum, dixit: "Fortasse, vita non solum est de muro et pugnis, sed etiam de his momentis laetis."

When they reached the camp, they all fell into their beds, tired but content. Gaius, before sleep, said: "Perhaps life is not only about the wall and battles, but also about these joyful moments."

Et in silentio noctis, sub luce stellarum, Gaius somniavit de vita plena et varia, etiam in extremis terrae Romanorum finibus.

And in the silence of the night, under the light of the stars, Gaius dreamed of a full and varied life, even at the farthest reaches of Roman lands.

Capitulum V: Exploratio Ultra Murum

Aurora adhuc obscura erat cum Gaius et alii milites, armis instructi, ad explorandum ultra Murum Hadriani profecti sunt. In silvam densam et tenebrosam intraverunt, foliis sub pedibus strepentibus.

Dawn was still dark when Gaius and the other soldiers, armed, set out to explore beyond Hadrian's Wall. They entered a dense and shadowy forest, with leaves rustling under their feet.

"Sequimur vestigia," inquit centurio, "forsitan barbarorum sunt." Vestigia in terra humida et lutea viderunt, caute sequentes.

"We are following tracks," said the centurion, "perhaps they belong to the barbarians." They saw tracks in the wet and muddy ground, cautiously following them.

Per silvam ambulantes, ad vallem pervenerunt. "Hic castra ponamus," dixit centurio. Tendis erectis, milites ad quidquid nox attulisset parati erant.

Walking through the forest, they reached a valley. "Let us set up camp here," said the centurion. With tents erected, the soldiers were ready for whatever the night might bring.

Noctu, cum ignes castrorum lucebant, sonos silvae audiebant. Gaius et amicus eius, Titus, ad ignem sedebant. "Audisti fabulam de lupo magnifico qui in his silvis habitat?" inquit Titus. Gaius, risum in oculis habens, respondit: "Narrare debes!"

At night, when the campfires were burning, they heard the sounds of the forest. Gaius and his friend, Titus, sat by the fire. "Have you heard the story of the magnificent wolf that lives in these woods?" asked Titus. Gaius, with laughter in his eyes, replied: "You must tell it!"

Titus fabulam de lupo, qui sapiens et fortis esset, narravit. Milites, fabulam audientes, simul ridebant et simul caute ad tenebras circumspiciebant.

Titus told the story of a wolf, who was wise and strong. The soldiers, hearing the story, laughed together while cautiously looking into the darkness around them.

Cum sol surgeret, iterum ambulaverunt. Silvae densae erant, sed milites fortiter procedebant. Flumen latum et rapidum invenerunt. "Transgredi debemus," inquit centurio.

When the sun rose, they walked again. The forests were dense, but the soldiers marched on bravely. They came upon a wide and swift river. "We must cross," said the centurion.

Trans flumen, aqua ad genua veniens, milites laboriose ambulaverunt. Gaius, aquam frigidam sentiens, dixit: "Frigidior aqua Romae non est!"

Across the river, with water reaching their knees, the soldiers trudged laboriously. Gaius, feeling the cold water, said: "The water in Rome is not this cold!"

Ultra flumen, in colle stantes, procul homines viderunt. "Barbari sunt," inquit centurio. "Observemus et intellegamus."

Beyond the river, standing on a hill, they saw people in the distance. "They are barbarians," said the centurion. "Let us observe and understand."

Gaius et alii milites barbaros observabant, qui ignes habebant et animalia coquebant. "Non videntur nos velle invadere," inquit Gaius.

Gaius and the other soldiers watched the barbarians, who had fires and were cooking animals. "They don't seem to want to attack us," said Gaius.

Sed subito, centurio signum dedit. "Revertamur," inquit. "Nobis satis intellegimus." Celeriter et silenter, ad murum redierunt.

But suddenly, the centurion gave the signal. "Let us return," he said. "We have understood enough." Quickly and quietly, they returned to the wall.

Cum ad murum pervenissent, centurio reportavit: "Barbari non sunt imminenti periculo." Gaius, muro stans, cogitavit de hominibus quos viderat. "Non omnes extra murum hostes sunt," susurravit.

When they reached the wall, the centurion reported: "The barbarians do not pose an imminent threat." Gaius, standing by the wall, thought about the people he had seen. "Not everyone beyond the wall is an enemy," he whispered.

Nocte illa, Gaius de exploratione et de rebus quas viderat et didicerat cogitavit. Stellae, sicut semper, super eum lucebant, et somnium pacis et concordiae inter Romanos et barbaros in corde eius crescebat.

That night, Gaius thought about the expedition and the things he had seen and learned. The stars, as always, shone above him, and a

dream of peace and harmony between Romans and barbarians grew
in his heart.

Capitulum VI: Adventus Barbarorum

Mane erat cum nuntius trepidus ad castra Romana cucurrit. "Barbari veniunt!" exclamavit. Gaius, qui iam in armis erat, ad alios milites se vertit. "Parati sumus," inquit.

It was morning when an anxious messenger ran to the Roman camp. "The barbarians are coming!" he exclaimed. Gaius, who was already armed, turned to the other soldiers. "We are ready," he said.

Centurio, vir gravis et fortis, milites ad murum duxit. "Arma et scuta capite," imperavit. Gaius, gladium suum stringens, de familia sua Romae cogitabat. "Pro illis pugnabo," sibi dixit.

The centurion, a serious and strong man, led the soldiers to the wall. "Take up your weapons and shields," he ordered. Gaius, drawing his sword, thought about his family in Rome. "I will fight for them," he said to himself.

Subito, a septentrione, barbarorum turmae apparuerunt. "Ecce hostes!" clamavit centurio. Milites, firmi et parati, ad pugnam steterunt.

Suddenly, from the north, groups of barbarians appeared. "Behold the enemy!" shouted the centurion. The soldiers, firm and ready, stood for battle.

Pugna incipit. Gaius, gladio et scuto armatus, in prima acie pugnabat. Clamores et sonus armorum aere resonabant.

The battle began. Gaius, armed with sword and shield, fought in the front line. Shouts and the sound of weapons echoed in the air.

Gaius, oculos plenos irae habens, fortiter pugnabat. Hostes, feroces et impetui pleni, contra Romanos ruebant. Sed Gaius et eius commilitones, disciplina et virtute, resistebant.

Gaius, with eyes full of fury, fought bravely. The enemies, fierce and full of attack, charged at the Romans. But Gaius and his comrades resisted with discipline and courage.

Interim, barbari ad murum propius et propius accesserunt. Gaius, scutum altius levans, hostes cum magna virtute repellebat. "Hodie," inquit, "murum nostrum defendemus!"

Meanwhile, the barbarians came closer and closer to the wall. Gaius, raising his shield higher, repelled the enemies with great strength. "Today," he said, "we will defend our wall!"

Pugna diu et acriter gerebatur. Gaius, vulneratus in brachio, tamen pugnabat. "Non desistam," sibi dixit. "Pro Roma et pro imperio!"

The battle was fought for a long time and fiercely. Gaius, wounded in the arm, still fought on. "I will not give up," he said to himself. "For Rome and for the Empire!"

Subito, cum sol ad meridiem esset, barbari, fatigati et repulsi, recesserunt. Gaius et alii milites, victoriosi, sed exhausti, super murum steterunt. "Vicimus," inquit Gaius, "pro Roma!"

Suddenly, when the sun was at noon, the barbarians, tired and driven back, retreated. Gaius and the other soldiers, victorious but exhausted, stood on the wall. "We have won," said Gaius, "for Rome!"

Post pugnam, Gaius et alii milites vulnera sua curabant. Gaius, fasciam circa brachium suum volvens, de barbaris cogitabat. "Quid illi volunt?" se interrogavit.

After the battle, Gaius and the other soldiers treated their wounds. Gaius, wrapping a bandage around his arm, thought about the barbarians. "What do they want?" he asked himself.

Nocte illa, victoria celebrabatur. Milites circa ignes sedebant, cibum et vinum habentes. Gaius, stellis in caelo fulgentibus aspiciens, dixit: "Hodie pro Roma pugnavimus. Sed spero pacem inter nos et barbaros aliquando futuram."

That night, the victory was celebrated. The soldiers sat around the fires, eating and drinking wine. Gaius, looking at the shining stars in the sky, said: "Today we fought for Rome. But I hope that one day there will be peace between us and the barbarians."

Et in silentio noctis, Gaius de pace et de futuro cogitabat. Stellae, sicut custodes aeterni, super eum lucebant, et somnia pacis et concordiae in mente eius volitabant.

And in the silence of the night, Gaius thought about peace and the future. The stars, like eternal guardians, shone above him, and dreams of peace and harmony flew through his mind.

Capitulum VII: Nix et Hiems

Hiems severa advenit. Nix candida et frigida de caelo decidebat, universa castra Romana operiens. Gaius, in muro stans, frigore tremebat. Nives magnas et silvas nive opertas videbat. "Roma," susurravit, "ubi nix rara est."

A harsh winter arrived. White and cold snow was falling from the sky, covering the entire Roman camp. Gaius, standing on the wall, was trembling with cold. He saw large snowdrifts and forests covered in snow. "Rome," he whispered, "where snow is rare."

In castris, ignis magnus ardebat. Milites circum ignem congregati, vestimenta calida gestabant. Gaius ad ignem accessit, manus ad calorem extendens.

In the camp, a large fire was burning. The soldiers gathered around the fire, wearing warm clothes. Gaius approached the fire, extending his hands toward the warmth.

"Hiems dura est," dixit Marcus, amicus Gaii, "sed fortes sumus." Gaius, calore ignis fruens, respondit: "Firmitas nostra in his difficilibus temporibus probatur."

"The winter is harsh," said Marcus, a friend of Gaius, "but we are strong." Gaius, enjoying the warmth of the fire, responded: "Our strength is tested in these difficult times."

Nix sine cessatione cadebat. Gaius, in tabernaculo suo sedens, fabulas de deis Romanis narrabat. "Audite," inquit, "de Marte, deo belli, qui semper fortitudinem et audaciam inspirat."

The snow was falling without stopping. Gaius, sitting in his tent, was telling stories about the Roman gods. "Listen," he said, "about Mars, the god of war, who always inspires strength and courage."

Milites, fabulis auditis, de diis et heroibus Romanis cogitabant. Gaius, fabulam finiens, dixit: "Sicut Mars, etiam nos fortes et invicti sumus."

The soldiers, having heard the stories, were thinking about the Roman gods and heroes. Gaius, finishing the story, said: "Like Mars, we too are strong and undefeated."

In tabernaculo, cibum et vinum habebant. Gaius, panem frangens, dixit: "Licet hiems sit dura, tamen calidum cibum et bonum vinum habemus. Pro salute nostra!"

In the tent, they had food and wine. Gaius, breaking bread, said: "Even though the winter is harsh, we still have warm food and good wine. For our health!"

Gaius, vinum bibens, de Roma cogitabat. "Quam pulchra est Roma vere et aestate," inquit. "Sed etiam in hieme, in his muris remotis, Roma in cordibus nostris est."

Gaius, drinking the wine, thought about Rome. "How beautiful Rome is in the spring and summer," he said. "But even in winter, on these distant walls, Rome is in our hearts."

Nocte, omnia in castris tranquilla erant. Gaius, in lecto suo iacens, stellas per nives lucere videbat. "Pax et tranquillitas," susurravit, "etiam in hieme, etiam in finibus imperii nostri, possunt inveniri."

At night, everything in the camp was peaceful. Gaius, lying in his bed, could see the stars shining through the snow. "Peace and tranquility," he whispered, "even in winter, even at the edges of our empire, can be found."

Et in silentio noctis, Gaius de pace et amore cogitabat, stellae supra nives fulgentes quasi signa spei et tranquillitatis. In corde Gaii, Roma semper erat, sicut stella clara in nocte hiemali.

And in the silence of the night, Gaius thought about peace and love, the stars shining above the snow like symbols of hope and tranquility. In Gaius's heart, Rome was always present, like a bright star on a winter night.

Capitulum VIII: Ludi in Castris

Dies festus in castris Romanis ad Murum Hadriani celebrabatur. Sol lucidus in caelo fulgebat, et omnes milites laetitiam et solacium exspectabant. "Hodie," inquit Gaius ad suos commilitones, "ludis et certaminibus fruemur!"

A festival day was being celebrated in the Roman camp at Hadrian's Wall. The bright sun was shining in the sky, and all the soldiers were expecting joy and comfort. "Today," Gaius said to his comrades, "we will enjoy games and competitions!"

In campo, prope castra, ludi et certamina incepta sunt. Cursus pedum, luctatio, et iactus disci inter varia certamina erant. Gaius, cursu pedum participans, lineam finalem primus transivit. "Victoria!" exclamavit, sudore et gaudio perfusus.

In the field near the camp, the games and competitions began. Foot races, wrestling, and discus throwing were among the various contests. Gaius, participating in the foot race, crossed the finish line first. "Victory!" he exclaimed, drenched in sweat and joy.

Milites et incolae, qui ad spectandum venerant, clamore magno Gaium celebrabant. "Gaius! Gaius!" clamabant, plaudentes.

The soldiers and villagers, who had come to watch, celebrated Gaius with loud cheers. "Gaius! Gaius!" they shouted, applauding.

Post certamina, cibum et vinum distributum est. Gaius, cum amicis suis sedens, panem et caseum edebat, vinumque rubrum bibebat. "Pro victoria et amicitia!" inquit, calicem suum tollens.

After the competitions, food and wine were distributed. Gaius, sitting with his friends, was eating bread and cheese, and drinking red wine. "To victory and friendship!" he said, raising his cup.

Cum omnes ederent et biberent, Gaius fabulam de Hercule, heroe magno Romanorum, coepit narrare. "Hercules," inquit, "multos labores fecit et semper fortis et audax fuit."

As everyone was eating and drinking, Gaius began to tell the story of Hercules, the great Roman hero. "Hercules," he said, "performed many labors and was always strong and brave."

Milites, fabula audita, de virtute et fortitudine cogitabant. Gaius, fabulam finiens, dixit: "Sicut Hercules, etiam nos fortes et invicti esse debemus."

The soldiers, after hearing the story, thought about virtue and strength. Gaius, finishing the story, said: "Like Hercules, we too must be strong and undefeated."

Musica incepit, citharistae et tibicines canebant. Saltatio et risus castra impleverunt. Omnes, milites et incolae, cum gaudio saltabant et ridebant.

Music began, and the lyre players and flute players were playing. Dancing and laughter filled the camp. Everyone, soldiers and villagers, danced and laughed with joy.

Gaius, in medio saltationis et musicae, sentiebat se vere felicem esse. "In his momentis," cogitavit, "vera laetitia et amicitia sunt."

Gaius, in the midst of the dancing and music, felt truly happy. "In these moments," he thought, "there is true joy and friendship."

Nocte, cum stellae in caelo fulgentes apparerent, Gaius ad castra rediit. Caelum stellatum contemplans, dixit: "In his stellis, pulchritudo et pax mundi nostri sunt."

At night, when the shining stars appeared in the sky, Gaius returned to the camp. Gazing at the starry sky, he said: "In these stars, there is beauty and peace in our world."

In castris, cum quiete et pace noctis, Gaius sentiebat se vere felicem esse. "In Romanis castris," inquit, "non solum pugnae et labor sunt, sed etiam laetitia et amicitia." Et sub lumine stellae, in nocte serena, Gaius somnia dulcia habebat, de diebus festis et momentis laetis in vita militari.

In the camp, with the quiet and peace of the night, Gaius felt truly happy. "In Roman camps," he said, "there is not only fighting and labor but also joy and friendship." And under the light of the stars, in the calm night, Gaius had sweet dreams of festival days and joyful moments in military life.

Capitulum IX: Epistula a Familia

In frigido mane ad Murum Hadriani, nuntius Gaium invenit et epistulam ei tradidit. "Ex Roma," inquit nuntius. Gaius, manibus tremulis, epistulam aperuit.

On a cold morning at Hadrian's Wall, a messenger found Gaius and handed him a letter. "From Rome," said the messenger. Gaius, with trembling hands, opened the letter.

Epistula, scripta manu matris suae, de vita in Roma et amicis narrabat. Gaius, legens, subridens cogitavit de calidis diebus Romae et de risu amicorum.

The letter, written by his mother's hand, told of life in Rome and his friends. Gaius, reading it, smiled and thought of the warm days in Rome and the laughter of friends.

Gaius, epistulam complectens, ad amicos suos in tabernaculo accessit. "Epistulam a familia accepi!" exclamavit. Amici, circum eum congregati, laeti erant audiendo de Roma et de familia Gaii.

Gaius, holding the letter close, went to his friends in the tent. "I received a letter from my family!" he exclaimed. His friends, gathered around him, were happy to hear about Rome and Gaius's family.

In tabernaculo, Gaius epistulam rursus legit, singula verba matris suae in corde suo tenens. "Quam dulcis est memoria familiae," inquit.

In the tent, Gaius read the letter again, holding every word from his mother in his heart. "How sweet is the memory of family," he said.

Gaius, de reditu Romam cogitans, ad murum ambulavit. Murum spectans, in animo suo imaginem urbis Romae et viarum eius vidit. "Quam velim redire," susurravit.

Gaius, thinking about returning to Rome, walked to the wall. Looking at the wall, he saw in his mind the image of the city of Rome and its streets. "How I wish to return," he whispered.

Stans super murum, Gaius epistulam ad familiam suam scribere coepit. De vita in castris, de frigore et nivibus, de amicis suis narrabat. "Vos desidero," scribebat.

Standing on the wall, Gaius began to write a letter to his family. He wrote about life in the camp, the cold and snow, and his friends. "I miss you," he wrote.

In epistula, Gaius de futuro et de spe sua Romam redire narravit. "Spero me mox vos visurum," scribebat. "Roma semper in corde meo est."

In the letter, Gaius spoke of the future and his hope to return to Rome. "I hope to see you soon," he wrote. "Rome is always in my heart."

Cum epistulam finivit, Gaius ad nuntium rediit et epistulam ei dedit. "Ad Romam," inquit. "Cura ut familia mea hoc legat."

When he finished the letter, Gaius returned to the messenger and gave him the letter. "To Rome," he said. "Make sure my family reads this."

Nocte illa, Gaius in tabernaculo suo iacebat, sollicitus de futuro. "Quid mihi et amicis meis erit?" cogitabat. "Quid de Roma?"

That night, Gaius lay in his tent, worried about the future. "What will become of me and my friends?" he thought. "What about Rome?"

Cum stellae in caelo fulgerent et luna clara esset, Gaius pacem in animo suo invenit. "Sive Romae sive hic," inquit, "vita semper nova est et plena spei." Et in silentio noctis, Gaius somnia dulcia de reditu Romam et ad familiares habebat.

As the stars shone in the sky and the moon was bright, Gaius found peace in his heart. "Whether in Rome or here," he said, "life is always new and full of hope." And in the silence of the night, Gaius had sweet dreams of returning to Rome and to his family.

Capitulum X: Reditus Romam

Cum aurora adhuc pallida esset, Gaius, miles Romanus, paratus erat Romam redire. Cor eius laetitia et tristitia mixtum erat. Diu ad Murum Hadriani militaverat, nunc autem tempus erat redire.

When dawn was still pale, Gaius, a Roman soldier, was ready to return to Rome. His heart was mixed with joy and sadness. He had served for a long time at Hadrian's Wall, but now it was time to return.

Amicos suos in castris salutavit. "Valete, amici," inquit Gaius. "Fortasse nos in Roma iterum videbimus." Milites, commilitones eius, eum complexi sunt. "Vale, Gaie," responderunt. "Felix sis in itinere tuo."

He greeted his friends in the camp. "Farewell, friends," said Gaius. "Perhaps we will see each other again in Rome." The soldiers, his comrades, embraced him. "Farewell, Gaius," they replied. "May you be lucky on your journey."

Iter longum et difficile ante eum erat. Per silvas densas et montes altos iter faciebat. Gaius, ambulans, de vita sua ad murum Hadriani cogitabat. De frigore, de pugnis, de amicis.

A long and difficult journey lay ahead of him. He traveled through dense forests and high mountains. Gaius, walking, thought about his life at Hadrian's Wall. About the cold, the battles, the friends.

Post multos dies, Gaius ad finem itineris sui appropinquavit. Colles et flumina familiaria videbat, et cor eius gaudio replebatur. "Roma," inquit, "domus mea."

After many days, Gaius approached the end of his journey. He saw familiar hills and rivers, and his heart was filled with joy. "Rome," he said, "my home."

Cum Romam pervenisset, porta urbis sub sole fulgente stetit. Familia eius eum laeta exceperat. Mater eum complexa est, pater manus eius tenuit. "Fili mi," dixerunt. "Quam felices sumus te redire!"

When he arrived in Rome, he stood at the city gate under the shining sun. His family joyfully welcomed him. His mother embraced him, and his father held his hands. "My son," they said. "How happy we are to have you back!"

Gaius, domi sedens, de rebus gestis suis narravit. De muris altis, de barbaris, de hieme dura. "Multa didici," inquit. "Fortis et sapiens factus sum."

Gaius, sitting at home, told stories of his deeds. About the tall walls, the barbarians, the harsh winter. "I have learned much," he said. "I have become strong and wise."

Nunc, in urbe Romana iterum habitabat. Viis eius ambulabat, fora et templa visitabat. "Quam pulchra est Roma," inquit. "Quam dulcis est vita hic."

Now, he was living in the city of Rome again. He walked through its streets, visited the forums and temples. "How beautiful Rome is," he said. "How sweet life is here."

Sed Gaius, cum in urbe ambularet, de futura vita in Roma cogitabat. "Quid nunc faciam?" se interrogavit. "Quo modo vitam meam agam?"

But Gaius, as he walked in the city, thought about his future life in Rome. "What will I do now?" he asked himself. "How will I live my life?"

Nocte, cum stellae in caelo fulgerent, Gaius de futuro suo cogitabat. Roma, cum omnibus suis possibilitatibus et spebus, ante eum iacebat. "Vitam novam incipiam," inquit. "Vitam plenam et felicem."

At night, when the stars were shining in the sky, Gaius thought about his future. Rome, with all its possibilities and hopes, lay before him. "I will begin a new life," he said. "A full and happy life."

Et cum somnus venisset, Gaius somniavit de vita nova in Roma, plena periculis et amicitia, plena pace et amore. Roma, urbs aeterna, nunc domus eius erat, plena futurorum promissionum.

And when sleep came, Gaius dreamed of a new life in Rome, full of dangers and friendship, full of peace and love. Rome, the eternal city, was now his home, full of promises for the future.

Certamina Currus in Circensibus Maximis

In urbe Roma antiqua, in loco celebri Circus Maximus appellato, populus ad spectandum certamina currūum frequentissime conveniebat. Circus Maximus locus longus et ovalis erat, locus amplus ubi ad ludos spectandos populus congregabatur. Hodie tibi de certaminibus currūum in ludis Circensibus in Circo Maximo narrabo.

In ancient Rome, in a famous place called the Circus Maximus, people very frequently gathered to watch chariot races. The Circus Maximus was a long and oval space, a large area where people gathered to watch games. Today I will tell you about the chariot races in the circus games at the Circus Maximus.

Prima luce, omnes ad Circum Maximum confluere coeperunt. Populus ex universa urbe Roma et finitimis regionibus ad spectaculum convenerat. Sol aureus in caelo fulgebat, et omnia pulchra erant.

At first light, everyone began to flock to the Circus Maximus. People from all over the city of Rome and nearby regions had gathered for the spectacle. The golden sun was shining in the sky, and everything was beautiful.

Circus erat lato in campo et alto in muro, marmore splendente ornatus. Homines quidam, aurigae appellati, in currus magnificos et veloces ascendebant. Currus duarum rotarum erant, aurigaeque pilis et vestibus splendidis induebantur. Equi, quibus currus iuncti erant, nervosi et veloces erant, et cum campanis sonantibus ornati.

The Circus was situated in a wide field and had high walls adorned with gleaming marble. Certain men, called charioteers, climbed into magnificent and swift chariots. The chariots had two wheels, and the charioteers wore bright helmets and clothing. The horses, which were harnessed to the chariots, were nervous and fast, adorned with jingling bells.

Spectatores in gradibus Circi Maximi sedebant, varia coloribus vestibus ornati. Mulieres, viri, et liberi omnes aderant, etiam imperator cum familia sua. Populus clamoribus et vocibus laetitiae omnia implebat.

Spectators sat in the tiers of the Circus Maximus, dressed in clothing of various colors. Women, men, and children were all present, even the emperor with his family. The people filled everything with cheers and joyful voices.

Primum certamen 'missio' vocabatur, quo aurigae per magnam orbitam currebant ut ordines suos servarent. Deinde, certamen verum et proprium incipiebat, 'ludi factionum' nominati. Erant nempe quattuor factiones aut collegia aurigarum: factiones Albata, Russata, Veneta, et Prasina.

The first race was called the "missio," where the charioteers ran around the large track to keep their positions. Then, the real and proper race began, called the "games of the factions." There were four factions or teams of charioteers: the white, red, blue, and green teams.

Aurigae factionum in currus suos ascendebant, et certamen incipiebat. Currus ad invicem competitorum concurrere debebant, et cursus erat longus et periculosus. Equi velocissimi ad lineam triumphalem currebant, ubi victor auream coronam accipiebat.

The charioteers of the factions climbed into their chariots, and the race began. The chariots had to compete against each other, and the race was long and dangerous. The fastest horses ran to the finish line, where the victor received a golden crown.

Populus favebat factioni suae, clamoribus et vocibus eos sustentans. Aurigae, qui victores erant, gloriam magnam et praemia accipiebant. Sed enim victoria non sine periculo erat, nam saepe currus collidebant et aurigae casus graves patiebantur.

The people cheered for their faction, supporting them with shouts and voices. The charioteers who were victorious received great glory and prizes. But victory was not without danger, for often the chariots would collide, and the charioteers would suffer serious accidents.

Interdum spectatores etiam alia ludos spectaculaque inter certamina currus spectabant. Erant elephantini, qui elephantos ingentes et mirabiles exhibebant. Etiam erant saltatores, qui saltus altos faciebant et fabulas agitabant.

Sometimes, spectators also watched other games and shows between the chariot races. There were elephant trainers, who exhibited giant and marvelous elephants. There were also acrobats, who performed high jumps and acted out stories.

Certamina currus per totum diem procedebant, et populus certaminibus omnibus libenter fruebatur. Cum sol occideret et stellae in caelo fulgerent, Circus Maximus lumine nocturno et clamoribus spectatorum fulgebat.

The chariot races continued throughout the entire day, and the people gladly enjoyed all the competitions. When the sun set and the stars shone in the sky, the Circus Maximus gleamed with night lights and the cheers of the spectators.

Hoc erat spectaculum magnificum et grandis occasio ludendi et celebrandi. Certamina currus in Circensibus Maximis Romanis memoriae nostrae testes sunt de splendore et laetitia Romae antiquae.

This was a magnificent spectacle and a great occasion for fun and celebration. The chariot races in the great Roman Circus games are a testament to the splendor and joy of ancient Rome in our memories.

Mirabilis Dies in Balneis Caracallae

Capitulum I: In Domo Divitis Romani

Romanus, patricius dives, in villa sua praeclara mane excitatur. "Salve, dies novus!" inquit et e lecto surgit. In triclinio leve prandium a servis ei paratur. "Parvum cibum ad me ferte," Romanus servis imperat. Dum edit, cogitat de consiliis diei.

A wealthy patrician Roman wakes up in his splendid villa in the morning. "Hello, new day!" he says and rises from bed. In the dining room, a light breakfast is prepared for him by the slaves. "Bring me a small meal," the Roman commands the slaves. While eating, he thinks about the plans for the day.

Post prandium, Romanus statuit se ad Balnea Caracallae ire ut relaxaretur. Balneum petiturus, sarcinam suam cum oleis et strigile parat. Tunicam simplicem, balneis aptam, induit.

After breakfast, the Roman decides to go to the Baths of Caracalla to relax. Preparing to visit the baths, he gathers his bag with oils and a strigil. He puts on a simple tunic suitable for the baths.

Romanus servos iubet ut iter ad balnea praeparent. Dum in pulchro suo horto ambulat, statuas et plantas admiratur. "Quam pulcher est hortus meus!" inquit.

The Roman orders his slaves to prepare for the journey to the baths. While walking in his beautiful garden, he admires the statues and plants. "How beautiful my garden is!" he says.

Deinde, villa sua relicta et paucis servis comitatus, iter ad Balnea Caracallae incipit. Per occupatas vias Romae ambulans, Romanus de vita Romana meditatur.

Then, leaving his villa and accompanied by a few slaves, he begins his journey to the Baths of Caracalla. Walking through the busy streets of Rome, the Roman reflects on Roman life.

Cum per vias ambulat, subito amicus eius Marcus occurrit. "Salve, Marce!" Romanus exclamat. "Quo vadis?" Marcus respondet, "Ego quoque ad Balnea Caracallae eo. Simul ibimus?"

As he walks through the streets, suddenly his friend Marcus meets him. "Hello, Marcus!" the Roman exclaims. "Where are you going?" Marcus replies, "I am also going to the Baths of Caracalla. Shall we go together?"

Romanus consentit et ambo ad balnea pergunt, de vita et rebus Romanis colloquuntur. Marcus de ludis gladiatoribus recentibus narrat, Romanus autem de novis aedificiis in urbe.

The Roman agrees, and both head to the baths, talking about life and Roman matters. Marcus talks about the recent gladiator games, while the Roman speaks about new buildings in the city.

Dum iter faciunt, tumultus in via oritur. Homines currunt et clamant. "Quid accidit?" Romanus rogat. Marcus respondet, "Videtur parva rixa inter mercatores esse." Curiosi, ad locum tumultus accedunt et spectant.

While they are walking, a commotion arises in the street. People are running and shouting. "What is happening?" the Roman asks. Marcus replies, "It seems to be a small fight between merchants." Out of curiosity, they approach the scene of the commotion and watch.

Duos mercatores de pretio pugnantes vident. Romanus, vir iustus, ad eos accedit et dicit, "Pacem inter vos facite! Nonne Romani estis?" Mercatores, Romanum respectantes, pugnam desistunt et ei gratias agunt.

They see two merchants fighting over a price. The Roman, a just man, approaches them and says, "Make peace between yourselves! Are you not Romans?" The merchants, respecting the Roman, stop the fight and thank him.

Post hanc actionem, Romanus et Marcus iter suum ad balnea continuant, de incidente et de pace Romana colloquuntur. Romanus sentit se non solum relaxationem quaerere, sed etiam partem esse magnae et variae urbis Romae.

After this action, the Roman and Marcus continue their journey to the baths, discussing the incident and Roman peace. The Roman feels that he is not only seeking relaxation but also a part of the great and diverse city of Rome.

Cum ad Balnea Caracallae perveniunt, Romanus et Marcus parati sunt diem in otio et amicitia fruendi.

When they arrive at the Baths of Caracalla, the Roman and Marcus are ready to enjoy the day in leisure and friendship.

Capitulum II: Iter ad Balneas

Romanus et Marcus, postquam a villa discesserunt, per vias Romae frequentatas ambulant. Homines variarum classium, mercatores, artificesque in viis apparent. "Quam varia est vita Romae!" inquit Romanus, populum spectans.

The Roman and Marcus, after leaving the villa, walk through the busy streets of Rome. People of various classes, merchants, and craftsmen appear in the streets. "How varied is life in Rome!" says the Roman, watching the people.

Dum ambulant, aromata culinae Romanae sensibus eorum obveniunt. "Olfac aromata ista!" hortatur Marcus. "Vera Roma in his odoribus est." Venditores cibum in viis vendentes vident, et breviter consistunt ut fructum emant.

As they walk, the aromas of Roman cuisine reach their senses. "Smell those aromas!" urges Marcus. "The real Rome is in these smells." They see vendors selling food in the streets and briefly stop to buy some fruit.

Mox ad Forum Romanum perveniunt, ubi fervet activitas politica. "Ecce Forum," inquit Romanus, "cor Romae." Homines togati, quasi actores in scaena, in foro apparent, orationes habentes.

Soon they arrive at the Roman Forum, where political activity is bustling. "Behold the Forum," says the Roman, "the heart of Rome." Men in togas, like actors on a stage, appear in the forum, giving speeches.

Iter continuantes, magnificas aedificationes Romanae mirantur. "Architectura nostra sine pari est," dicit Marcus. Romanus, assentiens, columnas et arcus admiratur.

As they continue their journey, they marvel at the magnificent Roman buildings. "Our architecture is without equal," says Marcus. The Roman, agreeing, admires the columns and arches.

Dum ambulant, Romanus cum servis suis colloquitur. "Cura ut nihil desit in sarcinis," inquit. Servi, diligenter audientes, promittunt omnia curata esse.

As they walk, the Roman speaks with his slaves. "Make sure nothing is missing from the baggage," he says. The slaves, listening carefully, promise that everything is taken care of.

Subito, pueri ludentes in via apparent. Pilam pilaque ludunt, risus et clamores eorum per vias resonantes. Romanus et Marcus paulisper consistunt, ludum spectantes et suae iuventutis memores.

Suddenly, boys playing in the street appear. They are playing with a ball, their laughter and shouts echoing through the streets. The Roman and Marcus stop for a moment, watching the game and remembering their own youth.

Deinde, ad flumen Tiberim perveniunt. Aqua fluminis sub sole micat, et ambo viri momentaneam tranquillitatem sentiunt. "Tiberis noster, urbis vita," inquit Romanus, flumen spectans.

Then they arrive at the river Tiber. The water of the river glistens under the sun, and both men feel a momentary peace. "Our Tiber, the life of the city," says the Roman, watching the river.

Prope finem itineris, magnificas Balneas Caracallae procul vident. "Ecce destinatio nostra!" exclamat Marcus. Romanus, balneas aspiciens, relaxationem iam sentit.

Near the end of their journey, they see the magnificent Baths of Caracalla in the distance. "Behold our destination!" exclaims Marcus. The Roman, looking at the baths, already feels relaxation.

Cum ad balneas appropinquant, conversatio inter Romanum et Marcum fit de expectationibus diei. "Hodie in balneis multa nova experiri possumus," inquit Romanus. Marcus, excitatus, consensit.

As they approach the baths, the conversation between the Roman and Marcus turns to the day's expectations. "Today we can experience many new things in the baths," says the Roman. Marcus, excited, agrees.

Tandem ad balneas perveniunt. Porta magnifica et muri alti balneas circumdant. "Iam tempus est intrare," dicit Marcus. Romanus, gaudio et expectatione plenus, ad portam balnearum accedit.

Finally, they arrive at the baths. A magnificent gate and high walls surround the baths. "Now it is time to enter," says Marcus. The Roman, full of joy and anticipation, approaches the gate of the baths.

Capitulum III: In Balneis Caracallae

Romanus et Marcus, cum ad Balneas Caracallae pervenerunt, magnam portam et magnificentiam admirantur. "Quam pulchrae sunt hae balneae!" inquit Romanus. Marcus nummulum parvum ad ostium dat, ut intrare possint.

The Roman and Marcus, when they arrived at the Baths of Caracalla, admired the grand gate and magnificence. "How beautiful these baths are!" said the Roman. Marcus handed a small coin at the entrance so they could enter.

Intrantes, turbam diversam conspiciunt – homines ex omnibus Romae partibus venientes. "Vide quam multi conveniunt ad hunc locum!" exclamat Marcus. Romanus, circumspiciens, caput annuit.

Upon entering, they saw a diverse crowd – people coming from all parts of Rome. "Look how many gather at this place!" exclaimed Marcus. The Roman, looking around, nodded his head.

Cum intrant, aer calidus et humidus eos salutat. "Iam vapores salubres sentio," inquit Romanus. Marcus ridet et consensit.

As they entered, the warm and humid air greeted them. "I can already feel the healthful vapors," said the Roman. Marcus laughed and agreed.

In apodyterio, Romanus vestimenta balnearia induit, vestes suas in loculo securi reponens. "Non possum exspectare ut relaxem," inquit, dum vestimenta mutat.

In the changing room, the Roman put on bathing clothes, securely placing his clothes in a locker. "I can't wait to relax," he said, while changing his clothes.

Deinde, ad palaestram procedunt, ubi levia exercitia incipiunt. Romanus et Marcus inter se iocantur, dum se ad balneum praeparant.

Then, they proceeded to the exercise area, where they began light exercises. The Roman and Marcus joked with each other as they prepared for the bath.

In palaestra, Romanus pilae ludum cum notis quibusdam incipit. Risus et clamores ludorum per aera resonant. "Haec est vera vita!" clamat Romanus, pilam iaciens.

In the exercise area, the Roman started a ball game with some acquaintances. Laughter and the shouts of the games echoed through the air. "This is the true life!" shouted the Roman, throwing the ball.

Dum ludunt, de novis rebus et politica Romae colloquuntur. "Audistine de recentibus senatus consiliis?" interrogat Marcus. Romanus, pilam capiens, respondet, "Etiam, multa in urbe nostra mutantur."

While they played, they talked about new events and Roman politics. "Have you heard about the recent decisions of the Senate?"

asked Marcus. The Roman, catching the ball, replied, "Yes, many things are changing in our city."

Ludo finito, Romanus sudore perfusus, sed hilaris est. "Nunc ad tepidarium procedamus," inquit. Marcus, fatigatus sed laetus, assentit.

With the game finished, the Roman, covered in sweat but cheerful, said, "Now let's go to the tepidarium." Marcus, tired but happy, agreed.

Ambulantes ad tepidarium, Romanus de variis balneis Romae loquitur. "Balneae non solum corpus curant, sed etiam animum," inquit. Marcus, iuxta eum ambulans, de balnearum philosophia cogitat.

As they walked to the tepidarium, the Roman spoke about the various baths in Rome. "The baths not only care for the body but also for the mind," he said. Marcus, walking beside him, thought about the philosophy of the baths.

Cum ad tepidarium perveniunt, Romanus et Marcus ad proximam experientiam parati sunt. "Hic vera relaxatio incipit," inquit Romanus, limen tepidarii transiens.

When they arrived at the tepidarium, the Roman and Marcus were ready for the next experience. "Here the true relaxation begins," said the Roman, crossing the threshold of the tepidarium.

Capitulum IV: Experientia Tepidarii

Romanus et Marcus, cum in tepidarium ingressi sunt, calorem lenem statim sentiunt. "Quam suavis est haec caliditas!" inquit Romanus, in subsellio marmoreo recumbens. Marcus similiter facit, et ambo viri relaxari incipiunt.

The Roman and Marcus, when they entered the tepidarium, immediately felt the gentle warmth. "How pleasant this warmth is!" said the Roman, reclining on a marble bench. Marcus did the same, and both men began to relax.

Dum iacent, amici ad eos accedunt, et colloquia incipiunt. "Salvete, amici!" exclamat Romanus. "Quid novi apud vos est?" Conversatio mox ad philosophiam et recentes Romae res vertitur.

As they lay there, friends approached them, and conversations began. "Greetings, friends!" exclaimed the Roman. "What's new with you?" The conversation soon turned to philosophy and recent events in Rome.

"Senatum novas leges considerare dicitur," quidam amicus narrat. Romanus, attentus, interrogat, "Quid de his legibus sentis?" Disputatio amica sed fervida oritur.

"The Senate is said to be considering new laws," one friend reported. The Roman, attentive, asked, "What do you think of these laws?" A friendly but heated discussion arose.

Interim, Romanus et Marcus mosaicos parietum et architecturam loci admirantur. "Videte quam artificiose haec omnia facta sunt," inquit Marcus, designa marmorea ostendens.

Meanwhile, the Roman and Marcus admired the mosaics on the walls and the architecture of the place. "Look how skillfully all of this was made," said Marcus, pointing to the marble designs.

Romanus oleum in cutem suam applicat, fragrantiam olei per tepidarium diffundens. "Hoc oleum cuti optimo est," inquit, suaviter se unguens.

The Roman applied oil to his skin, spreading the fragrance of the oil throughout the tepidarium. "This oil is excellent for the skin," he said, gently anointing himself.

Deinde servus advenit et Romanum leniter massat. "Quam placidum hoc est!" suspirat Romanus, manuum expertarum servuli usu fruens.

Then a servant arrived and gently massaged the Roman. "How soothing this is!" sighed the Roman, enjoying the skillful hands of the servant.

Circumstantium aquae murmur et hominum colloquia auditu iucunda sunt. "Hic locus quasi paradisus est," inquit Marcus, ambientis sonos audiens.

The murmur of surrounding water and the conversations of people were pleasant to hear. "This place is like paradise," said Marcus, listening to the sounds of the surroundings.

Post haec, Romanus se refrigeratum et ad novum balneum paratum esse sentit. "Iam tempus est ad caldarium ire," inquit, surgens. Marcus assentit, "Ita, ad calidiores aquas nunc eamus."

After this, the Roman felt refreshed and ready for a new bath. "Now it's time to go to the caldarium," he said, rising. Marcus agreed, "Yes, let's go to the hotter waters now."

Cum ad caldarium accedunt, Romanus et Marcus ad calorem intensiorem experiri parati sunt. "Nunc ad calidissimas aquas procedimus," dicit Romanus, limen caldarii transiens.

As they approached the caldarium, the Roman and Marcus were ready to experience the more intense heat. "Now we proceed to the hottest waters," said the Roman, crossing the threshold of the caldarium.

Capitulum V: Experientia Caldarii

Romanus et Marcus, post tepidarium, in caldarium intrant. Calor intensus eos statim tangit. "Quam vehemens est hic calor!" exclamat Romanus, se in aquam calidam immergens. Marcus sequitur, et ambo in aqua relaxantur.

The Roman and Marcus, after the tepidarium, enter the caldarium. The intense heat touches them immediately. "How strong this heat is!" exclaims the Roman, immersing himself in the hot water. Marcus follows, and both relax in the water.

Dum in aqua sedent, amici ad eos accedunt, et colloquia philosophica incipiunt. "Quid de virtute cogitatis?" interrogat amicus quidam. Mox disputatio profunda et seria oritur, cum amici varias opiniones afferunt.

While they sit in the water, friends approach them, and philosophical discussions begin. "What do you think about virtue?" asks a certain friend. Soon, a deep and serious debate arises, as the friends offer various opinions.

In hoc colloquio, Romanus et Marcus vaporem et laquearia alta caldarii observant. "Mirum est, quam ingeniose haec aedificata sunt," inquit Marcus, laquearium admirans.

In this conversation, the Roman and Marcus observe the steam and the high ceilings of the caldarium. "It is amazing how ingeniously this was built," says Marcus, admiring the ceiling.

Momento silentii, Romanus ad reflexionem se vertit. "Interdum, in silentio, maxime cum me ipso loquor," inquit, oculos claudens.

In a moment of silence, the Roman turns to reflection. "Sometimes, in silence, I speak most with myself," he says, closing his eyes.

Colloquium deinde ad recentes ludi gladiatorii et certamina currus vertitur. "Nuper in Circo Maximo spectacula cursuum fuerunt," narrat Marcus. Romanus, audiendo, de periculo et audacia aurigarum cogitat.

The conversation then turns to recent gladiatorial games and chariot races. "Recently, there were races at the Circus Maximus," Marcus tells. The Roman, listening, thinks about the danger and bravery of the charioteers.

In caldario, Romanus purificationem profundam pororum experitur. "Hae aquae calidae poros purgant," inquit, sudorem de corpore suo sentiens.

In the caldarium, the Roman experiences a deep cleansing of his pores. "This hot water cleanses the pores," he says, feeling the sweat coming from his body.

The sensation of sweat and impurities leaving his body pleases the Roman. "Sweating here is healthy," he says, moving in the water.

Gradatim, Romanus et Marcus calori assuefiunt, seque renovatos sentiunt. "Hic calor non solum corpus, sed etiam animum reficit," dicit Romanus.

Gradually, the Roman and Marcus become accustomed to the heat, and they feel renewed. "This heat refreshes not only the body but also the mind," says the Roman.

Post aliquod tempus in caldario, Romanus statuit ad frigidarium movendum esse. "Nunc ad aquas frigidas transeamus," inquit. Marcus, caloribus vivificatus, consensit, "Ita, frigidarium nos exspectat."

After some time in the caldarium, the Roman decides it is time to move to the frigidarium. "Now let's move to the cold waters," he says. Marcus, invigorated by the heat, agrees, "Yes, the frigidarium awaits us."

Cum ad frigidarium accedunt, parati sunt ad novam experientiam temperaturae contrariae. "Nunc a calidis ad frigidas aquas transeamus," dicit Romanus, ad frigidarium ingressus.

As they approach the frigidarium, they are ready for a new experience of contrasting temperatures. "Now let's move from the hot to the cold waters," says the Roman, entering the frigidarium.

Capitulum VI: Experientia Frigidarii

Romanus et Marcus, post calorem caldarii, in frigidarium ingrediuntur. Frigus subitum eos statim tangit. "Heu! Quam frigidum est!" Romanus exclamat, in aquam frigidam ingressus. Marcus eum sequitur, et ambo viri frigore perterriti sunt.

The Roman and Marcus, after the heat of the caldarium, enter the frigidarium. The sudden cold touches them immediately. "Oh! How cold it is!" exclaims the Roman, stepping into the cold water. Marcus follows him, and both men are startled by the cold.

Paulatim tamen temperaturae mutationi assuescunt et se vivificatos sentiunt. "Nunc vires redire sentio," Marcus inquit, aqua frigida se reficiens.

Gradually, however, they become accustomed to the change in temperature and feel rejuvenated. "Now I feel my strength returning," says Marcus, refreshing himself in the cold water.

Romanus in aqua natat, musculos suos exercens. Marcus, ridens, eum sequitur, et ambo in aqua ludunt.

The Roman swims in the water, exercising his muscles. Marcus, laughing, follows him, and both play in the water.

Dum natant, amici eos iocis de frigore salutant. "Vos in hac aqua videre, mirum est!" amicus clamat. Romanus et Marcus cum risu respondet, iocos amicorum fruentes.

While they swim, their friends greet them with jokes about the cold. "Seeing you in this water is amazing!" a friend shouts. The Roman and Marcus reply with laughter, enjoying their friends' jokes.

In frigidario, Romanus et Marcus frescos parietum et sculpturas admirantur. "Arte nostra non solum in aedificiis, sed etiam in balneis utimur," Romanus inquit, opera artis spectans.

In the frigidarium, the Roman and Marcus admire the frescoes on the walls and the sculptures. "We use our art not only in buildings but also in baths," says the Roman, looking at the works of art.

Interim, cum aliis balneatoribus iocos leves et colloquia amica habent. "Frigus post calorem bonum est," Romanus ad balneatorem iuxta se inquit. Ille ridet et consensit.

Meanwhile, they share light jokes and friendly conversations with other bathers. "The cold after the heat is good," the Roman says to a bather next to him. He laughs and agrees.

Romanus sentit musculos suos contrahi et sensus acui. "Frigus corpus firmat," inquit, se in aqua movens.

The Roman feels his muscles contracting and his senses sharpening. "The cold strengthens the body," he says, moving through the water.

Dum in frigidario sunt, Romanus de equilibrio inter therapiae calidae et frigidae cogitat. "Calor relaxat, frigus confirmat," inquit, philosophiam balnearum considerans.

While they are in the frigidarium, the Roman reflects on the balance between hot and cold therapies. "Heat relaxes, cold strengthens," he says, considering the philosophy of the baths.

Sentit etiam sensum communionis et amicitiae in balneis. "Hic omnes pares sumus, in aqua," Marcus inquit, circumspiciens. Romanus assentit, "Balnea non solum de corpore, sed etiam de societate sunt."

He also feels a sense of community and friendship in the baths. "Here, we are all equals, in the water," says Marcus, looking around. The Roman agrees, "The baths are not only about the body, but also about society."

Post aliquod tempus in frigidario, Romanus statuit ad proximam activitatem transire. "Nunc tempus est hinc discedere," inquit. Marcus, refectus, surgit, paratus ad novam experientiam.

After some time in the frigidarium, the Roman decides to move on to the next activity. "Now it's time to leave," he says. Marcus, refreshed, rises, ready for a new experience.

Capitulum VII: Activitates Sociales et Otiosae

Post experientias in caldario et frigidario, Romanus et Marcus sese siccant et tunicas novas induunt. "Nunc ad alia loca balnearum eamus," inquit Romanus, paratus ad novas activitates.

After their experiences in the caldarium and frigidarium, the Roman and Marcus dry themselves and put on fresh tunics. "Now let's go to other places in the baths," says the Roman, ready for new activities.

Primum ad bibliothecam balnearum pergunt. Ibi, Romanus et Marcus volumina historiae et poesiae legunt. "Quam multa discere possumus!" inquit Marcus, pergamenum evolvens.

First, they go to the library of the baths. There, the Roman and Marcus read volumes of history and poetry. "How much we can learn!" says Marcus, unrolling a parchment.

Dum in bibliotheca sunt, Romanus cum erudito viro de historia Romae disputat. "Credo historiam Romanam maximam esse," affirmat Romanus, argumenta sua proferens.

While in the library, the Roman debates Roman history with a learned man. "I believe Roman history to be the greatest," the Roman asserts, presenting his arguments.

Postea, ad popinam balnearum vadunt, ubi ficus et caseum degustant. "Quam bona sunt haec!" exclamat Marcus, ficum edens.

Afterwards, they go to the baths' café, where they taste figs and cheese. "How good these are!" exclaims Marcus, eating a fig.

Deinde, ludum tabularem, latrunculis similem, cum amico ludunt. Ludus est acutus, et ambo viri in strategia se exercent. "Bonus lusor es," dicit Romanus amico suo, ridens.

Then, they play a board game similar to chess with a friend. The game is sharp, and both men exercise themselves in strategy. "You are a good player," says the Roman to his friend, laughing.

Dum ludunt, coetus musicorum prope incipit pergere. Melodiae dulces et rhythmi per auras fluitant. "Musica in balneis vera delectatio est," inquit Romanus, musicis auscultans.

While they play, a group of musicians begins to perform nearby. Sweet melodies and rhythms float through the air. "Music in the baths is a true delight," says the Roman, listening to the music.

Post ludum, Romanus et Marcus cum amicis levem cenam sumunt, de vita familiaris colloquuntur. "Familia fundamentum vitae Romanae est," asserit Romanus, panem frangens.

After the game, the Roman and Marcus have a light meal with friends, talking about family life. "Family is the foundation of Roman life," asserts the Roman, breaking bread.

Deinde, in hortis balnearum placide ambulant. Plantae et flores mirum colorem et odorem praeferunt. "Horti nos ad naturam revocant," inquit Marcus, flores spectans.

Then, they walk peacefully in the gardens of the baths. The plants and flowers offer wonderful color and fragrance. "The gardens bring us back to nature," says Marcus, watching the flowers.

Dum in hortis ambulant, Romanus de visitatione theatri post balneas cogitat. "Hodie ad theatrum eamus," inquit. "Spectacula post balneas iucunda sunt."

While walking in the gardens, the Roman thinks about visiting the theater after the baths. "Let's go to the theater today," he says. "Performances after the baths are enjoyable."

Marcus consensit, "Spectaculum videre post balneas perfectum est." Ambo viri, post diem plenum in balneis actum, ad theatrum ire parati sunt.

Marcus agreed, "Seeing a show after the baths is perfect." Both men, after a full day spent in the baths, are ready to go to the theater.

Capitulum VIII: Rituum Olei et Strigilis

Postquam in hortis balnearum ambulaverunt, Romanus et Marcus ad ritum olei et strigilis se praeparant. Romanus oleum in corpus suum iterum applicat, ad purgandum paratus. "Hoc oleum corpus purgabit," inquit.

After walking in the gardens of the baths, the Roman and Marcus prepare themselves for the ritual of oil and the strigil. The Roman applies oil to his body again, ready for cleansing. "This oil will cleanse the body," he says.

Deinde strigilem adhibet ad sordes, oleum, et sudorem a corpore suo detrahendum. Marcus idem facit, et ambo viri se modo mundo purificant.

Then he uses the strigil to remove dirt, oil, and sweat from his body. Marcus does the same, and both men purify themselves in this traditional way.

Postquam sordes detrahit, Romanus se mundatum et exfoliatum sentit. "Quam purus nunc sum!" inquit, cutem suam laudans.

After removing the dirt, the Roman feels cleansed and exfoliated. "How pure I am now!" he says, praising his skin.

Facientes hoc, de beneficiis huius ritus cum amicis colloquuntur. "Hic ritus non solum corpus, sed etiam animum purgat," Romanus asserit. Amici consentiunt, ritum laudantes.

While doing this, they discuss the benefits of the ritual with friends. "This ritual cleanses not only the body but also the mind," the Roman asserts. The friends agree, praising the ritual.

Dum hoc agunt, alios in eodem ritu occupatos observant. Homines diversi status et aetatis strigilibus utuntur, communis ritus participes.

As they perform this, they observe others engaged in the same ritual. People of different status and ages use strigils, participating in a common tradition.

Romanus aqua oleum reliquum abluit, se puriorem tam corpore quam mente sentiens. "Aqua haec ultimum purgationis gradum perficit," inquit.

The Roman washes off the remaining oil with water, feeling purer in both body and mind. "This water completes the final step of cleansing," he says.

Hoc facto, Romanus de importantia huius ritus in cultura Romana cogitat. "Curatio corporis pars vitae Romanae est," secum ipse reputans.

With this done, the Roman reflects on the importance of this ritual in Roman culture. "The care of the body is a part of Roman life," he thinks to himself.

Interim, amicum novum in ritu strigilis iuvat. "Sic strigili utere," demonstrat Romanus amico, usum strigilis explicans.

Meanwhile, he helps a new friend in the use of the strigil. "Use the strigil like this," the Roman demonstrates to his friend, explaining its use.

Postquam ritum perfecerunt, Romanus et Marcus ad locum requietis se praeparant. "Nunc tempus est ad requiem," inquit Romanus, relaxatus et purgatus.

After completing the ritual, the Roman and Marcus prepare themselves for a place of rest. "Now it is time to rest," says the Roman, relaxed and purified.

Capitulum IX: In Area Requiei et Colloquia Ultima

Post ritum olei et strigilis, Romanus et Marcus in area requiei se collocant, in lectis mollibus recumbentes. "Hic vere quiescere possumus," inquit Romanus, in lecto se accommodans.

After the ritual of oil and strigil, the Roman and Marcus settle themselves in the resting area, reclining on soft couches. "Here we can truly rest," says the Roman, adjusting himself on the couch.

Cum amicis suaviter colloquuntur, fabulas leves et iocos inter se communicantes. "Hodie in balneis multa gavisi sumus," dicit Marcus, risum partiens.

They chat pleasantly with friends, sharing light stories and jokes with each other. "We have enjoyed many things in the baths today," says Marcus, sharing a laugh.

Romanus de familia sua et rebus gestis narrat. "Filii mei nuper multa in schola didicerunt," inquit cum gaudio paterno. Amici, audientes, eum laudant et suas historias communicant.

The Roman talks about his family and recent accomplishments. "My sons have recently learned much in school," he says with paternal joy. His friends, listening, praise him and share their own stories.

Amici de itineribus et rebus gestis suis narrare incipiunt. "Nuper Graeciam navigavi," quidam amicus dicit. Romanus et Marcus, intenti, fabulas peregrinationum audiunt.

The friends begin to talk about their travels and achievements. "I recently sailed to Greece," says a friend. The Roman and Marcus, listening intently, hear stories of these journeys.

Dum colloquuntur, servus potum refrigerantem affert. Romanus et Marcus bibunt, "Quam reficiens est hoc!" exclamat Romanus, potionem fruens.

While they are talking, a servant brings a refreshing drink. The Roman and Marcus drink, "How refreshing this is!" exclaims the Roman, enjoying the drink.

In hoc loco, Romanus sensum relaxationis et contenti sentit. "In his balneis animus et corpus vere reficiuntur," inquit, oculos claudens.

In this place, the Roman feels a sense of relaxation and contentment. "In these baths, both the mind and body are truly restored," he says, closing his eyes.

Per apertum tectum, solem occidentem vident. "Quam pulcher est hic aspectus!" inquit Marcus, caelum aspiciens. Romanus, solem spectans, de diei fine cogitat.

Through the open roof, they see the setting sun. "How beautiful this view is!" says Marcus, looking at the sky. The Roman, watching the sun, thinks about the end of the day.

Dum requiescunt, de futuris conventibus et coetibus socialibus consiliantur. "Forte cras ad cenam conveniamus," suadet Romanus. Amici consensum dant, de futura nocte laeti.

As they rest, they plan future gatherings and social meetings. "Perhaps we can meet for dinner tomorrow," suggests the Roman. The friends agree, happy about the upcoming evening.

Romanus momenti sumit ut luxuriam balnearum aestimet. "Quam fortunati sumus, qui huius loci frui possumus," inquit, circumspiciens. Marcus, circumspiciens, luxuriam loci agnoscit.

The Roman takes a moment to appreciate the luxury of the baths. "How fortunate we are to enjoy this place," he says, looking around. Marcus, also looking around, acknowledges the luxury of the place.

Post haec, Romanus statuit tempus esse domum revertendi. "Hodie satis fructi sumus," inquit. "Nunc ad domos nostras redeamus." Marcus, contentus et refectus, surgit, paratus domum ire.

After this, the Roman decides it is time to return home. "We have enjoyed ourselves enough today," he says. "Now let us return to our homes." Marcus, content and refreshed, gets up, ready to go home.

Capitulum X: Ex Balneis Discedens et Domum Revertens

Romanus et Marcus, post diem in balneis Caracallae actum, res suas colligunt et vestes iterum induunt. "Quam bene hodie egimus," inquit Romanus, sarcinam suam componens.

The Roman and Marcus, after spending the day at the Baths of Caracalla, gather their things and put their clothes back on. "How well we did today," says the Roman, packing his bag.

Antequam exirent, gratias balnearum ministris et operariis agunt. "Gratias vobis agimus pro servitio vestro," dicit Romanus, eos salutans.

Before they leave, they thank the bath attendants and workers. "We thank you for your service," says the Roman, greeting them.

Balneas exeuntes, se renovatos et relaxatos sentiunt. "Hic dies vere reficiens fuit," inquit Marcus, limen balnearum transiens.

Leaving the baths, they feel renewed and relaxed. "This day was truly refreshing," says Marcus, crossing the threshold of the baths.

Dum domum sub caelo stellato Romano redeunt, de diei fructibus cogitant. "Quam multa hodie gavisi sumus," inquit Romanus, stellas aspiciens.

As they return home under the starry Roman sky, they reflect on the day's pleasures. "How much we enjoyed today," says the Roman, looking at the stars.

Romanus de diei experientiis in mente revolvit, cogitans quomodo eas cum familia sua participare possit. "Familia mea gaudet audire de his," inquit, de narrationibus futuris cogitans.

The Roman reflects on the day's experiences, thinking about how he can share them with his family. "My family will be glad to hear about this," he says, thinking of future stories.

Dum ambulant, Romanus de aliis balneis Romae celebribus visitandis cogitat. "Forte ad alias balneas Romae ire debebimus," inquit, de novis locis explorandis cogitans.

As they walk, the Roman thinks about visiting other famous baths in Rome. "Perhaps we should visit other Roman baths," he says, thinking of exploring new places.

Sensum superbiae in cultura et societate Romana sentit. "Roma non solum urbs est, sed etiam cultura," inquit, de magnitudine Romae reputans.

He feels a sense of pride in Roman culture and society. "Rome is not just a city, but a culture," he says, reflecting on the greatness of Rome.

Cum ad domum suam perveniunt, a familia calide salutantur. "Salvete! Rediimus!" exclamat Romanus, ostium aperiens. Familia eum et Marcum benigne excipit.

When they arrive at his home, they are warmly greeted by the family. "Greetings! We have returned!" exclaims the Roman, opening the door. The family kindly welcomes him and Marcus.

Romanus, diem consummatus, ad cubiculum suum se recipit, de futuris visitationibus ad balneas cogitans. "Iterum ad balneas venire desidero," inquit, in lecto suo recumbens.

The Roman, after a fulfilling day, retreats to his room, thinking about future visits to the baths. "I wish to come to the baths again," he says, reclining in his bed.

De Viis Romanis

In antiqua Roma, viae magnae aedificatae sunt. Viae Romanae longae et firmatae erant. Romani vias ad multas partes imperii sui fecerunt.

In ancient Rome, great roads were built. Roman roads were long and reinforced. The Romans built roads to many parts of their empire.

Prima via Romana "Via Appia" nominata est. Via Appia a Roma ad Brundisium ducit. Haec via valde celeberrima est. Via Appia lapidibus et saxis strata est.

The first Roman road was named the "Via Appia." The Via Appia leads from Rome to Brundisium. This road is very famous. The Via Appia is paved with stones and rocks.

Romae, multae viae sunt. Viae rectae et bene constructae sunt. In viis, milites, mercatores, et cives ambulant. Viae Romanae ad omnes partes Italiae ducunt.

In Rome, there are many roads. The roads are straight and well-constructed. On the roads, soldiers, merchants, and citizens walk. Roman roads lead to all parts of Italy.

Viae Romanae non solum in Italia sunt, sed etiam in aliis terris. In Gallia, Hispania, Graecia, et Africa viae sunt. Viae ad omnes provincias Romani imperii ducunt.

Roman roads are not only in Italy, but also in other lands. In Gaul, Spain, Greece, and Africa, there are roads. Roads lead to all the provinces of the Roman Empire.

In via, tabellae sunt. Tabellae viatoribus monstrant quam longe ad urbem veniant. Tabellae utiles ad iter faciendum sunt.

On the road, there are signs. The signs show travelers how far they are from the city. The signs are useful for making journeys.

Ad vias, pontes et tunnella sunt. Romani pontes lapideos aedificant. Tunnelia montes transeunt. Opera Romana ingeniosa sunt.

Along the roads, there are bridges and tunnels. The Romans build stone bridges. Tunnels pass through mountains. Roman works are ingenious.

Viae commercio sunt magni momenti. Mercatores in viis ambulant. Mercatores cibum, vestes, et alia bona portant. Commercium sine viis difficile est.

Roads are very important for trade. Merchants walk on the roads. Merchants carry food, clothes, and other goods. Trade is difficult without roads.

Militibus viae etiam utiles sunt. Milites cito in imperio ambulant. Milites ad loca longinqua ire possunt. Viae ad defendendum imperium necessariae sunt.

Roads are also useful for soldiers. Soldiers march quickly across the empire. Soldiers can travel to distant places. Roads are necessary for defending the empire.

Romani etiam mansiones ad vias aedificant. Mansiones loca sunt ubi viatores quiescunt. In mansionibus viatores dormiunt et cibum edunt.

The Romans also build inns along the roads. Inns are places where travelers rest. In inns, travelers sleep and eat food.

Viae Romanae ad historiam et culturam Romanam magnae sunt. Vias Romanae hodie videre possumus. Viae Romanorum admirationem nostram habent.

Roman roads are great for Roman history and culture. Today, we can still see Roman roads. The roads of the Romans have our admiration.

De Aquaeductibus Romanis

In Roma antiqua, aquaeductus magni erant. Aquaeductus aquam ad urbes portabant. Romani aquaeductus bene aedificaverunt.

In ancient Rome, aqueducts were large. Aqueducts carried water to the cities. The Romans built aqueducts well.

Romani primum aquaeductum fecerunt. Aquaeductus ex locis longinquis veniebant. Aqua in urbem per aquaeductus fluebat. Aquaeductus lapidibus magnis constructi sunt.

The Romans made the first aqueduct. The aqueducts came from distant places. Water flowed into the city through the aqueducts. The aqueducts were constructed from large stones.

Aquaeductus non solum in Roma erant, sed etiam in aliis terris Romani imperii. In Hispania, Gallia, et Africa aquaeductus erant. Per aquaeductus, aqua ad multas urbes perveniebat.

Aqueducts were not only in Rome but also in other lands of the Roman Empire. In Spain, Gaul, and Africa, there were aqueducts. Through aqueducts, water reached many cities.

Aquaeductus alti et longi erant. Saepe aquaeductus per valles et colles ibant. In montibus, aquaeductus per tunnella ducebantur. Opera Romana ingeniis magnis facta sunt.

Aqueducts were tall and long. Often, aqueducts went through valleys and hills. In the mountains, aqueducts were carried through tunnels. Roman works were made with great engineering skill.

Aquaeductus ad vitam urbanam necessarii erant. Per aquaeductus, aqua ad balneas, fontes, et domos portabatur. Sine aquaeductibus, urbes Romanae non facile viverent.

Aqueducts were necessary for urban life. Through aqueducts, water was brought to baths, fountains, and houses. Without aqueducts, Roman cities would not easily survive.

Romani aquam puram et clarum amabant. Aquam ex aquaeductibus bibebant. Romani in aqua pura lavabant. Aquaeductus ad salutem populi Romani erant.

The Romans loved pure and clear water. They drank water from the aqueducts. The Romans bathed in pure water. Aqueducts were essential for the health of the Roman people.

Interdum, aquaeductus reparari debebant. Romani aquaeductus diligenter custodiebant. Si aquaeductus frangebantur, cito reparabantur.

Sometimes, aqueducts had to be repaired. The Romans carefully maintained the aqueducts. If the aqueducts broke, they were quickly repaired.

Hodie, multa aquaeductus Romani adhuc stant. Aquaeductus antiqui magnitudinem Romani ingenii ostendunt. Gentes hodie aquaeductus Romanos mirantur.

Today, many Roman aqueducts still stand. Ancient aqueducts show the greatness of Roman engineering. People today admire the Roman aqueducts.

Iter Romanorum: Aelii et Iulii Facinoribus

Capitulum I: Ex Roma Proficiscuntur

Aelius et Julius Romae in parva domo iuxta Forum Romanum habitant. Amici ab infantia sunt et multa simul faciunt. Hodie autem dies novus et excitans est.

Aelius and Julius live in a small house near the Roman Forum. They have been friends since childhood and do many things together. However, today is a new and exciting day.

"Amice," Aelius ad Julium dicit, "hodie incipimus iter nostrum ad Londinium! Multa mira videbimus."

"Friend," Aelius says to Julius, "today we begin our journey to London! We will see many wonders."

Julius ridet et respondet, "Ita vero, Aelie! Multas terras et maria transibimus. Spero nos multas periculas habituros esse!"

Julius laughs and replies, "Indeed, Aelius! We will cross many lands and seas. I hope we will face many adventures!"

Ambulantes per vias Romae, ad tabernam veniunt ubi sarcinas suas colligunt. Sarcinae sunt graves, sed animi eorum leves sunt propter iter.

Walking through the streets of Rome, they come to a tavern where they collect their bags. The bags are heavy, but their spirits are light because of the journey.

"Vale, mater!" Aelius clamat. Julius similiter manum matris suae tenet et dicit, "Vale, cara mater, mox reveniemus."

"Goodbye, mother!" Aelius shouts. Julius similarly holds his mother's hand and says, "Goodbye, dear mother, we will return soon."

Cum sol altus in caelo est, per viam Appiam ambulant. Via est pulchra et plena historiae. Caelum serenum est, et sol calidus lucet.

When the sun is high in the sky, they walk along the Appian Way. The road is beautiful and full of history. The sky is clear, and the sun shines warmly.

"Vide, Aelie!" Julius exclamat, "Quam pulchra est Roma nostra!"

"Look, Aelius!" Julius exclaims, "How beautiful our Rome is!"

"Etiam, sed Londinium quoque pulchrum erit," Aelius respondet. "Quid inveniemus, nescimus."

"Indeed, but London will also be beautiful," Aelius responds. "What we will find, we do not know."

Post multas horas ambulant, in tabernam prope viam intrant. Ibi, breviter requiescunt, aquam bibunt, et panem edunt. Risus et colloquia sunt undique in taberna.

After many hours of walking, they enter a tavern near the road. There, they rest briefly, drink water, and eat bread. Laughter and conversations fill the tavern.

"Salve, amici," tabernarius dicit. "Unde venitis et quo itis?"

"Hello, friends," the tavernkeeper says. "Where are you from and where are you going?"

"Ex Roma sumus," Julius respondet. "Et nunc Londinium iter facimus."

"We are from Rome," Julius replies. "And now we are traveling to London."

"O, longum iter!" tabernarius exclamat. "Cavete viam, nonnumquam latrones sunt!"

"Oh, a long journey!" the tavernkeeper exclaims. "Beware the road, sometimes there are robbers!"

Subito, dum Aelius panem mordet, fur ad eum accedit et sacculum rapit. Aelius clamorem non audit quia panem edit.

Suddenly, while Aelius is biting his bread, a thief approaches him and steals his bag. Aelius does not hear the shout because he is eating bread.

Julius autem, qui videt omnia, statim clamat, "Fur! Fur! Aelie, sacculum tuum rapit!"

But Julius, who sees everything, immediately shouts, "Thief! Thief! Aelius, he is stealing your bag!"

Aelius statim surgit et, "Quid? Ubi est?" exclamat.

Aelius immediately stands up and exclaims, "What? Where is it?"

Julius, celeriter surgens, "Illic! Furrite!" clamat. Ambo currunt post furem, qui per vias tortuosas fugit.

Julius, rising quickly, shouts, "There! Run after him!" Both run after the thief, who flees through winding streets.

Fur celer est, sed Aelius et Julius celeriores sunt. Per vias Romae currunt, et homines in via clamant et mirantur.

The thief is fast, but Aelius and Julius are faster. They run through the streets of Rome, and people shout and wonder in the streets.

"Capite furem!" aliquis clamat.

"Catch the thief!" someone shouts.

Post breve tempus, Aelius furem apprehendit et sacculum suum recuperat. Fur territus est et, "Ignoscite mihi!" clamat.

After a short time, Aelius catches the thief and recovers his bag. The thief is terrified and shouts, "Forgive me!"

"Cur nos furaris?" Julius severus interrogat.

"Why did you steal from us?" Julius asks sternly.

Fur respondet, "Pauper sum et esurio. Ignoscite mihi, quaeso!"

The thief responds, "I am poor and hungry. Please forgive me!"

Julius, misericordia motus, nummos in manum furem dat et dicit, "Tibi dono hos nummos. Noli amplius furari!"

Julius, moved by mercy, gives coins into the thief's hand and says, "I give you these coins. Do not steal again!"

Fur, gratus et paenitens, discedit. Aelius et Julius, sacculum recuperati, iterum ad tabernam redeunt. Tabernarius, omnia videns, ridet et dicit, "Vos vere fortes et audaces estis! Fortuna vobiscum sit in itinere!"

The thief, grateful and repentant, leaves. Aelius and Julius, having recovered the bag, return to the tavern. The tavernkeeper, seeing everything, laughs and says, "You are truly brave and bold! May fortune be with you on your journey!"

Aelius et Julius, post hoc excitatum eventum, iterum sarcinas suas sumunt et iterum iter ad Londinium facere incipiunt. Sol iam occidit, et stellae in caelo lucere incipiunt. Roma eorum post tergum est, et periculae magnae ante eos iacent.

Aelius and Julius, after this exciting event, once again pick up their bags and begin their journey to London. The sun has already set, and the stars are starting to shine in the sky. Rome is behind them, and great dangers lie ahead.

Capitulum II: Periculum in Via

Aelius et Julius per viam festinant, Londinium petentes. Sol iam altus in caelo est, et calor diurnus sentitur.

Aelius and Julius hurry along the road, heading toward London. The sun is already high in the sky, and the heat of the day is felt.

"O Aelie, quam calidum est hodie!" Julius dicit, sudorem a fronte detergens.

"Oh Aelius, how hot it is today!" Julius says, wiping the sweat from his forehead.

"Etiam, Iuli, sed per illam silvam ambulabimus. Forsitan frigidior ibi erit," Aelius respondet, silvam densam et obscuram ostendens.

"Yes, Julius, but we will walk through that forest. Perhaps it will be cooler there," Aelius replies, pointing to the dense and dark forest.

Intrant in silvam, ubi umbra arborum grata est. Tamen locus satis obscurus et secretus videtur.

They enter the forest, where the shade of the trees is pleasant. However, the place seems quite dark and secluded.

"Haec silva valde densa est," Julius cautus dicit. "Oculos apertos habeamus."

"This forest is very dense," Julius says cautiously. "Let's keep our eyes open."

Dum per silvam ambulant, subito latrones ex arbustis exsiliunt! Aelius et Julius valde terrentur.

While walking through the forest, suddenly robbers jump out from the bushes! Aelius and Julius are very frightened.

"Nummos et sacculas vestras nobis date!" latro minitans clamat.

"Give us your coins and bags!" the robber shouts threateningly.

Aelius et Julius, perterriti, stant immobiliter. Latrones gladios habent et minaces apparent.

Aelius and Julius, terrified, stand still. The robbers have swords and appear menacing.

Julius, astute cogitans, latronibus ait: "Amici, nos pauperes sumus et nihil pretiosum habemus. Nummos paucos et cibum tantum."

Julius, thinking cleverly, says to the robbers: "Friends, we are poor and have nothing valuable. Just a few coins and some food."

Latro, Iulium audiens, paulum dubitat. Aelius, Iulii astutiam intellegens, addit: "Longo itinere sumus. Londinium imus. Nihil nobis est praeter has sarcinas."

The robber, hearing Julius, hesitates a bit. Aelius, understanding Julius's cleverness, adds: "We are on a long journey. We are going to London. We have nothing but these bags."

Alter latro exclamat: "Nonne estis Romani? Romani semper divites sunt!"

Another robber exclaims: "Aren't you Romans? Romans are always rich!"

Julius tamen ait: "Multi Romani pauperes sunt. Nos inter illos numeramur. Et si nos spoliatis, nihil boni invenietis."

Julius, however, says: "Many Romans are poor. We are among them. And if you rob us, you will find nothing of value."

Latrones inter se aspiciunt, dubitantes. Julius et Aelius, adhuc timidi, exspectant.

The robbers look at each other, uncertain. Julius and Aelius, still fearful, wait.

Tandem latrones dicunt: "Bene, vos relinquemus. Sed caveatis! Aliae viae periculosae sunt." Deinde in silvam discedunt.

Finally, the robbers say: "Fine, we will leave you. But be careful! Other roads are dangerous." Then they disappear into the forest.

Aelius et Julius, latrones abeuntes spectantes, levantur. "O Iuli, quam astute locutus es!" Aelius laetans dicit.

Aelius and Julius, watching the robbers leave, feel relieved. "Oh Julius, how cleverly you spoke!" Aelius says joyfully.

"Fortuna nobiscum fuit, Aelie. Sed nunc, celerius eamus," Julius respondet.

"Fortune was with us, Aelius. But now, let's go faster," Julius replies.

Ambulant celeriter per silvam, solliciti ne iterum latrones occurrant. Silva tandem finitur, et iter apertum ante eos patet.

They walk quickly through the forest, worried that they might encounter the robbers again. Finally, the forest ends, and an open road lies ahead of them.

Cum sol occidit et caelum obscuratur, ad villam perveniunt. Villa parva est, sed hospitium promittit.

As the sun sets and the sky darkens, they arrive at a villa. The villa is small, but it promises shelter.

"Salve, domine!" Aelius villanum salutans ait. "Hospitium quaerimus nocte hac."

"Hello, sir!" Aelius says, greeting the villa owner. "We seek shelter for this night."

Villanus, homo amicabilis, respondet: "Salvete, peregrini! Hospitium vobis do. Venite!"

The villa owner, a friendly man, replies: "Welcome, travelers! I offer you shelter. Come in!"

Aelius et Julius, grati et fatigati, villam intrant. Cenam simplicem sumunt et de periculis diei colloquuntur.

Aelius and Julius, grateful and tired, enter the villa. They have a simple meal and talk about the dangers of the day.

"Quam mirabile est iter nostrum iam!" Aelius dicit. "Pericula, latrones, et nunc tutum hospitium."

"How amazing our journey has been already!" Aelius says. "Dangers, robbers, and now safe shelter."

"Verum est," Julius addit. "Et multa adhuc ante nos sunt. Dormiamus nunc, cras novum diem habebimus."

"That's true," Julius adds. "And many things still lie ahead of us. Let's sleep now, tomorrow will bring a new day."

Et sic, in villa rustica, sub tecto simplici, Aelius et Julius, amici Romani, dormiunt. Somnia eorum aventuris et spe Londinium tandem pervenire plena sunt.

And so, in a rustic villa, under a simple roof, Aelius and Julius, Roman friends, sleep. Their dreams are full of adventures and the hope of finally reaching London.

Capitulum III: Navigatio Turbulenta

Aelius et Julius, post pericula silvae, ad portum Massiliae tandem perveniunt. Portus magnus est, plenus navibus et mercatoribus.

Aelius and Julius, after the dangers of the forest, finally arrive at the port of Massilia. The port is large, full of ships and merchants.

"Ecce, Iuli, quam magnus hic portus est!" Aelius exclamat, magnitudinem navium admirans.

"Look, Julius, how large this port is!" Aelius exclaims, admiring the size of the ships.

"Etiam, Aelie, multae viae maritimae hic incipiunt," Julius respondet, navem quaerens quae Londinium petat.

"Yes, Aelius, many sea routes begin here," Julius responds, looking for a ship bound for London.

Ambulantes per portum, navem Londinium petentem tandem inveniunt. Navis magna et robusta est, ad longum mare transgrediendum parata.

Walking through the port, they finally find a ship bound for London. The ship is large and sturdy, ready to cross the vast sea.

"Nautae, salvete!" Julius ad nautas navis clamat. "Ad Londinium navigatis?"

"Sailors, greetings!" Julius shouts to the sailors on the ship. "Are you sailing to London?"

"Etiam, ad Londinium! Vultisne nobiscum navigare?" nauta, amicabilis, respondet.

"Yes, to London! Do you want to sail with us?" a friendly sailor responds.

Aelius et Julius in navem ascendunt. Mare tranquillum est, et caelum serenum. Navis a portu solvitur et in mare magnum navigat.

Aelius and Julius board the ship. The sea is calm, and the sky is clear. The ship sets sail from the port and heads out into the vast sea.

"O Iuli, quam pulchrum mare est!" Aelius dicit, aquam caeruleam et serenam spectans.

"Oh Julius, how beautiful the sea is!" Aelius says, gazing at the blue and peaceful water.

"Sed mare saepe est fallax, Aelie. Semper parati esse debemus," Julius, cautus, addit.

"But the sea is often deceptive, Aelius. We must always be prepared," Julius adds cautiously.

Non multo post, subito venti fortissimi surgunt! Mare incipit turbare, et navis vehementer fluctuat.

Not long after, suddenly very strong winds arise! The sea begins to swell, and the ship rocks violently.

"Nautae, quid agemus?" Julius clamat, dum navis magis magisque movetur.

"Sailors, what shall we do?" Julius shouts, as the ship moves more and more.

"Nautae laborate! Vos fortes manete!" nauta maior clamat, gubernaculum tenens.

"Sailors, work hard! Stay strong!" the chief sailor shouts, holding the helm.

Aelius, mare spectans, valde nauseatur et pallidus fit. "O Iuli, male mihi est..." Aelius debiliter dicit.

Aelius, watching the sea, becomes very nauseous and turns pale. "Oh Julius, I feel sick..." Aelius says weakly.

"Forti animo esto, Aelie. Tempestas transibit," Julius, Aelium consolans, dicit, eum firmiter tenens.

"Be strong, Aelius. The storm will pass," Julius says, comforting Aelius and holding him firmly.

Tempestas autem peior fit. Undae altissimae sunt, et venti vehementissimi. Nautae valde laborant, navem stabilire conantes.

But the storm worsens. The waves are very high, and the winds are very strong. The sailors work hard, trying to stabilize the ship.

"Ne timete! Navis nostra fortis est!" nauta maior clamat, sed omnes in navis periculo sunt.

"Do not fear! Our ship is strong!" the chief sailor shouts, but everyone on the ship is in danger.

Post horas longas et terribiles, tempestas tandem desinit. Mare iterum tranquillum fit, et sol rursus lucet.

After long and terrible hours, the storm finally ends. The sea becomes calm again, and the sun shines once more.

"Gratias deo maris! Salvati sumus!" Aelius, relevatus, exclamat.

"Thank the god of the sea! We are saved!" Aelius exclaims, relieved.

"Mirabile est, quomodo mare cito mutatur," Julius dicit, adhuc cautus.

"It's amazing how quickly the sea changes," Julius says, still cautious.

Nautae, nunc laeti, navem ad Britanniam dirigunt. Mare placidum est, et navis tuto navigat.

The sailors, now happy, steer the ship towards Britain. The sea is calm, and the ship sails safely.

Cum ad litus Britannicum appropinquant, Aelius et Julius terra firma laetantur. "Britannia! Tandem!" exclamant.

As they approach the British shore, Aelius and Julius rejoice at the sight of solid land. "Britain! Finally!" they exclaim.

Navis ad litus appropinquat, et Aelius et Julius, post pericula maris, gaudium adventus magni sentiunt. In Britannia nova pars itineris eorum incipit, terra ignota et plena novarum aventurarum.

The ship approaches the shore, and Aelius and Julius, after the dangers of the sea, feel great joy at their arrival. In Britain, a new part of their journey begins, in an unknown land full of new adventures.

Capitulum IV: In Hospitio

Aelius et Julius, post navigationem turbulentam, ad hospitium Dubris perveniunt. Dubris est parvus vicus Britannicus, tranquillus et rusticus.

Aelius and Julius, after a turbulent voyage, arrive at an inn in Dubris. Dubris is a small British village, peaceful and rustic.

"En hospitium!" Aelius laetus exclamat. "Post diem longum et mare turbidum, quies nobis bona erit."

"Look, an inn!" Aelius exclaims happily. "After a long day and a rough sea, rest will be good for us."

"Intramus et cenam quaeramus," Julius suadet. Ambulant ad tabernam iuxta hospitium sitam.

"Let's go in and look for dinner," Julius suggests. They walk to a tavern next to the inn.

In taberna, multi homines bibunt et loquuntur. Aelius et Julius locum quietum quaerunt ubi sedent et cenam sumunt.

In the tavern, many people are drinking and talking. Aelius and Julius look for a quiet place where they can sit and eat dinner.

"Panis et pisces hodie sunt," tabernarius dicit, cibum in mensam ponens.

"Today we have bread and fish," the tavern keeper says, placing the food on the table.

Dum edunt, homo ebrius ad mensam eorum accedit. "Qui estis vos?" ebrius clamat, vultu turbato.

While they are eating, a drunk man approaches their table. "Who are you?" the drunk shouts with a troubled face.

"Sumus peregrini, pacifice hic cenamus," Julius respondet, pacem servare conatur.

"We are travelers, peacefully dining here," Julius responds, trying to keep the peace.

"Silenium! Nolo peregrinos hic!" ebrius iratus exclamat et pugnum movet.

"Silence! I don't want strangers here!" the drunk angrily exclaims and raises his fist.

Cito, rixa in taberna oritur. Homines clamant et pugnant. Julius et Aelius, periculo consci, effugere conantur.

Quickly, a fight breaks out in the tavern. People shout and fight. Julius and Aelius, aware of the danger, try to escape.

"Duc nos foras, Aelie!" Julius clamat, inter homines pugnantes se movens.

"Lead us out, Aelius!" Julius shouts, moving through the fighting crowd.

Aelius sequitur, et ambo celeriter ex taberna effugiunt, in noctem tenebrosam.

Aelius follows, and both quickly escape from the tavern into the dark night.

"In hospitium redeamus. Hic non tutum est," Aelius suadet, anhelans.

"Let's return to the inn. It's not safe here," Aelius suggests, panting.

In hospitio, in cubiculum suum intrant et in lectis per silente nocte dormiunt.

At the inn, they enter their room and sleep through the silent night in their beds.

Mane, cum sol oritur, Aelius et Julius surgunt. "Hodie iter nostrum pergitur," Aelius dicit, fenestram apertam spectans.

In the morning, as the sun rises, Aelius and Julius get up. "Today, our journey continues," Aelius says, looking out the open window.

"Primum, commeatus emamus. Cibus et aqua nobis necessarii sunt," Julius respondet.

"First, let's buy provisions. We need food and water," Julius replies.

Ambulant per viam vicus ad mercatum ubi mercatores vendunt. Multa venalia sunt: cibum, vestimenta, aliaque utilia.

They walk through the village road to the market where merchants are selling. Many things are for sale: food, clothing, and other useful items.

"Ecce, mercator qui panem et caseum vendit," Julius monet, ad tabernam mercatoris accedens.

"Look, a merchant selling bread and cheese," Julius points out, approaching the merchant's stall.

"Salve, mercator. Panem et caseum, quaeso," Aelius dicit, nummos in manum mercatoris ponens.

"Hello, merchant. Bread and cheese, please," Aelius says, placing coins into the merchant's hand.

Mercator eis cibum dat, et amici sacculos suos cibo implent.

The merchant gives them the food, and the friends fill their bags with provisions.

"Ecce etiam, aquam et vinum emamus," Julius suadet, ad aliam tabernam accedens.

"Let's also buy water and wine," Julius suggests, approaching another stall.

Cum commeatus emunt, parati sunt iter suum pergere. "Nunc ad Londinium iter nostrum ducit," Aelius dicit, viam versus Londinium spectans.

After buying provisions, they are ready to continue their journey. "Now, our path leads to London," Aelius says, looking down the road toward London.

"Multae res nobis manent exspectandae," Julius addit, cum amico ambulans.

"Many things still await us," Julius adds, walking with his friend.

Et sic, Aelius et Julius iter suum in Britannia pergunt, novis locis et hominibus occurrentes. Londinium adhuc longe est, sed animi eorum fortes et parati ad omnia sunt.

And so, Aelius and Julius continue their journey in Britain, encountering new places and people. London is still far away, but their spirits are strong and ready for anything.

Capitulum V: Per Silvam

Aelius et Julius, post hospitium in Dubris, iter per silvam densam incipiunt. Silva magna est, plena arborum altorum et umbrarum obscurarum.

Aelius and Julius, after their stay in Dubris, begin their journey through a dense forest. The forest is vast, full of tall trees and dark shadows.

"Densa haec silva est, sed per hanc viam iter nostrum est," Julius dicit, ramum a via movens.

"This forest is dense, but our path leads through it," Julius says, moving a branch from the path.

"Silvae semper mysteria habent," Aelius respondet, circumspiciens. "Audisne animalia silvestria?"

"Forests always hold mysteries," Aelius replies, looking around. "Do you hear the wild animals?"

"Sane," Julius dicit. "Lupi et ursi in hac silva esse possunt."

"Of course," Julius says. "Wolves and bears could be in this forest."

Subito, ante eos, lupus repente apparet! Est magnus et griseus, oculi eius in amicos fixi.

Suddenly, a wolf appears before them! It is large and gray, its eyes fixed on the friends.

"Immobiles maneamus," Julius susurrat, lupum intentus spectans.

"Let's stay still," Julius whispers, watching the wolf intently.

Aelius, tremens, "Quid faciemus si nos adgreditur?" timide interrogat.

Aelius, trembling, timidly asks, "What will we do if it attacks us?"

"Si non movemur, fortasse abibit," Julius respondet, lupi motus observans.

"If we don't move, perhaps it will leave," Julius responds, observing the wolf's movements.

Lupus eos paulum spectat, deinde sine nocendo in silvam abit. Aelius et Julius, magno cum timore, respirant.

The wolf watches them for a moment, then leaves into the forest without harm. Aelius and Julius, greatly relieved, breathe again.

"Fortuna nobiscum est, lupus nos non laesit," Aelius dicit, iterum incipiens ambulare.

"Fortune is with us, the wolf did not harm us," Aelius says, starting to walk again.

"Verum," Julius addit. "Sed deinceps magis cauti ambulemus."

"True," Julius adds. "But from now on, let's walk more carefully."

Ambulant per silvam, cautiores quam antea. Subito, ad fontem aquae purae perveniunt.

They walk through the forest, more cautious than before. Suddenly, they come upon a spring of clear water.

"Ecce, aqua!" Aelius exclamat. "Sitim leniamus."

"Look, water!" Aelius exclaims. "Let's quench our thirst."

"Prudentes simus, aquam prius inspiciamus," Julius monens dicit.

"Let's be careful, let's inspect the water first," Julius says, giving a warning.

Aquam inspectant, clara et pura videtur. Ambo aquam bibunt, sitim sedantes.

They inspect the water; it seems clear and pure. Both drink the water, quenching their thirst.

"Dulcis et frigida est," Aelius laetus dicit.

"It's sweet and cold," Aelius says happily.

"Dona naturae," Julius addit, aquam rursus bibens.

"Nature's gifts," Julius adds, drinking the water again.

Dum bibunt, caelum incipit obnubilari. Nubes griseae solis lucem operiunt.

While they are drinking, the sky begins to cloud over. Gray clouds cover the sunlight.

"Pluvia venire potest," Julius dicit, nubes spectans.

"Rain might come," Julius says, watching the clouds.

"Vestimenta nostra protegamus," Aelius respondet, sarcinam suam aperiens.

"Let's protect our clothes," Aelius responds, opening his pack.

Non multum post, pluvia levis incipit cadere. Guttae aquae in foliis arborum tintinnant.

Not long after, a light rain begins to fall. Water droplets tinkle on the leaves of the trees.

"Bene est," Aelius dicit. "Pluvia silvae sonum pulchrum facit."

"It's nice," Aelius says. "The rain makes a beautiful sound in the forest."

"Sed via nostra difficilior fit," Julius monet. "Lutum et aqua sunt."

"But our path becomes harder," Julius warns. "There is mud and water."

"Fortiter pergimus," Aelius dicit, per viam lutosam ambulans.

"We march on bravely," Aelius says, walking through the muddy path.

Per silvam ambulant, sub pluvia levi, naturae sonos audiunt. Silva, quamquam densa et obscura, eis pulchra et pacifica videtur.

They walk through the forest under light rain, listening to the sounds of nature. Although dense and dark, the forest seems beautiful and peaceful to them.

Iter per silvam longum est, sed amici, una ambulantes, non despondent. Naturae pulchritudinem admirantur, etiamsi viam difficiliorem facit. Londinium adhuc longe est, sed cor eorum spe plenum est.

The journey through the forest is long, but the friends, walking together, do not lose heart. They admire the beauty of nature, even though it makes their path harder. London is still far away, but their hearts are full of hope.

Capitulum VI: Ad Flumen

Aelius et Julius, postquam silvam peractam attingunt, ad flumen latum perveniunt. Flumen rapidum est, aqua eius fortiter fluit.

Aelius and Julius, after completing the forest, reach a wide river. The river is swift, its water flows strongly.

"Ecce flumen!" Aelius dicit, ad aquam spectans. "Sed ubi pons est?"

"Look, a river!" Aelius says, looking at the water. "But where is the bridge?"

"Ibi est," Julius respondet, digitum ad pontem veterem et fragilem ostendens.

"There it is," Julius responds, pointing to an old and fragile bridge.

Pons ligneus est, vetustate consumptus. Tabulae eius non firmae videntur.

The wooden bridge is worn by age. Its planks do not seem sturdy.

"Caute transire debemus," Julius monet. "Pons hic periculosus videtur."

"We must cross carefully," Julius warns. "This bridge looks dangerous."

"Etiam, lente et caute," Aelius assentitur, primum gradum in pontem faciens.

"Yes, slowly and carefully," Aelius agrees, taking the first step onto the bridge.

Ambulant lente, tabulae sub pedibus eorum stridentes. Ventus flumen superfluit, sonum aquae augens.

They walk slowly, the planks creaking under their feet. The wind blows over the river, increasing the sound of the water.

Subito, cum in medio ponte sunt, tabula sub Aelio crepat! Aelius exclamat et in aquam cadit.

Suddenly, when they are in the middle of the bridge, a plank under Aelius cracks! Aelius shouts and falls into the water.

"Aelie!" Julius clamat, ad eum tendens. "Tene manum!"

"Aelius!" Julius shouts, reaching out to him. "Grab my hand!"

Aelius in aqua natat, conatus caput supra aquam tenere. "Iuli, adiuva me!"

Aelius swims in the water, trying to keep his head above the surface. "Julius, help me!"

Julius, sine cunctatione, in aquam desilit et Aelium apprehendit. Fortiter natat, Aelium ad ripam trahens.

Julius, without hesitation, jumps into the water and grabs Aelius. He swims strongly, pulling Aelius to the shore.

Finaliter, ambo in ripa exsistunt, anhelantes et madidi.

Finally, both of them reach the riverbank, gasping and soaked.

"Gratias tibi, Iuli," Aelius dicit, aquam ex vestimentis exprimens. "Vitam meam servasti."

"Thank you, Julius," Aelius says, squeezing water from his clothes. "You saved my life."

"Amici pro amicis semper," Julius respondet, subridens. "Sed nunc, vestimenta nostra sunt madida."

"Friends always help friends," Julius responds, smiling. "But now, our clothes are soaked."

"Et sarcina mea in flumine!" Aelius lamentatur, ad flumen spectans ubi sarcina eius natat.

"And my bag is in the river!" Aelius laments, looking at the river where his bag is floating.

"Res non bonae sunt, sed saltem vivimus," Julius consolatur.

"Things aren't great, but at least we're alive," Julius consoles him.

Sub arbore magna prope ripam requiescunt, vestimenta eorum ad solem siccantes. Sole occidente, iterum pergunt, sarcinis levioribus propter damnum.

They rest under a large tree near the bank, drying their clothes in the sun. As the sun sets, they continue on, with lighter bags due to the loss.

"Nunc, Londinium citius perveniemus," Julius iocatur, in viam praecedens.

"Now, we'll reach London faster," Julius jokes, leading the way.

"Si alia flumina non transibimus!" Aelius addit, ambo ridentes.

"If we don't cross any more rivers!" Aelius adds, and both laugh.

Ambulant sub stellis, cor eorum levius factum post periculum superatum. Londinium, finis itineris, in mente eorum manet, spes et fortitudo eos ducens.

They walk under the stars, their hearts lightened after overcoming the danger. London, the end of their journey, remains in their minds, with hope and strength guiding them.

Capitulum VII: In Mercatu

Aelius et Julius, post pericula fluminis, ad magnum mercatum in proxima urbe perveniunt. Mercatus est plenus tabernis et mercatoribus, qui omnia genera mercium vendunt.

Aelius and Julius, after the dangers of the river, arrive at a large market in the nearby city. The market is full of stalls and merchants, selling all kinds of goods.

"Quam multae res hic sunt!" Aelius admirans exclamat. "Omnia quae iter nostrum iuvare possunt."

"How many things there are here!" Aelius exclaims in admiration. "Everything that can help our journey."

"Primum, novas vestes emere debemus," Julius dicit, madidas suas vestes spectans. "Et fortasse cibum et aquam."

"First, we need to buy new clothes," Julius says, looking at his wet clothes. "And perhaps food and water."

Ambulant inter tabernas, multas merces spectantes. Fructus, panes, vestes, et multa alia venalia sunt.

They walk among the stalls, looking at many goods. Fruits, bread, clothes, and many other things are for sale.

Subito, dum Julius mercem spectat, fur tacite advenit et sacculum Julii furatur! Aelius, qui prope stat, furem videt et clamat, "Iuli, fur sacculum tuum rapit!"

Suddenly, while Julius is looking at goods, a thief silently approaches and steals Julius's bag! Aelius, who is standing nearby, sees the thief and shouts, "Julius, the thief is stealing your bag!"

Julius convertit et fur currens videt. "Eum persequamur!" exclamat.

Julius turns and sees the thief running. "Let's chase him!" he exclaims.

Aelius celeriter post furem currit. Fur per turbam mercati fugit, sed Aelius eum non amittit.

Aelius quickly runs after the thief. The thief flees through the crowded market, but Aelius does not lose him.

"Capite furem!" Aelius clamans currit. Homines in mercatu consistunt et spectant.

"Catch the thief!" Aelius shouts as he runs. People in the market stop and watch.

Tandem, Aelius furem apprehendit et cum eo luctatur. Sacculum Julii recuperat et fur captus est.

Finally, Aelius catches the thief and wrestles with him. He recovers Julius's bag, and the thief is caught.

"Hic est qui sacculum meum rapuit!" Julius adveniens dicit, ad furem iratus.

"This is the one who stole my bag!" Julius says as he arrives, angry at the thief.

"Hoc non iterum faciam," fur dicit, metu plenus.

"I won't do this again," the thief says, full of fear.

Aelius et Julius sacculum inspiciunt, et omnia intacta sunt. "Gratias tibi, Aelie, propter audaciam tuam," Julius dicit, amico gratias agens.

Aelius and Julius inspect the bag, and everything is intact. "Thank you, Aelius, for your bravery," Julius says, thanking his friend.

"Amicus semper alterum adiuvat," Aelius respondet, subridens.

"A friend always helps another," Aelius replies, smiling.

Postea, ad mercatorem accedunt, qui furtum vidit et adprehensionem furi adiuvit. "Gratias vobis agimus," Julius dicit. "Pro gratitudine nostra, aliquid ememus."

Afterwards, they approach a merchant who saw the theft and helped catch the thief. "We thank you," Julius says. "In gratitude, we will buy something."

Novas vestes emunt, sicut et cibum et aquam. Mercatoribus argentum solvunt et mercatum reliquias spectant.

They buy new clothes, as well as food and water. They pay the merchants and look around the market once more.

"Ecce, quam pulchrae sunt hae tunicae!" Aelius dicit, novas tunicas probans.

"Look, how beautiful these tunics are!" Aelius says, trying on the new tunics.

"Et utiliores erunt in itinere nostro," Julius addit, novam tunicam induens.

"And they will be more useful on our journey," Julius adds, putting on a new tunic.

Post emptiones, ad cauponam prope mercatum ambulant, ubi cenam capiunt. Cenam bonam edunt, de itinere suo colloquuntur.

After shopping, they walk to a nearby inn, where they have dinner. They eat a good meal and talk about their journey.

"Hodie, multa passi sumus," Aelius dicit. "Furtum, persecutionem, et nunc quies in hac caupona."

"Today, we have endured a lot," Aelius says. "A theft, a chase, and now rest in this inn."

"Vera dicis," Julius respondet. "Iter nostrum multas res inexpectatas habet, sed fortiter eas superamus."

"You speak the truth," Julius replies. "Our journey has many unexpected things, but we overcome them with strength."

Nocte, post cenam, iter ad proximam urbem faciunt. Sub lumine lunae et stellis, iterum ambulant, spe pleni quod Londinium mox attingent. Cor eorum plenum est audacia et amicitia, quae eos per omnes difficultates ducit.

At night, after dinner, they continue their journey to the next town. Under the light of the moon and stars, they walk again, full of hope that they will soon reach London. Their hearts are full of courage and friendship, which guide them through all difficulties.

Capitulum VIII: In Agris

Aelius et Julius, post tumultum mercati, iter suum per agros et campos Britanniae pergunt. Agri vasti sunt, pleni frugibus et pecoribus.

Aelius and Julius, after the chaos of the market, continue their journey through the fields and plains of Britain. The fields are vast, full of crops and livestock.

"Quam pulchra est haec terra," Aelius in ambulatu dicit, campos virides spectans.

"How beautiful this land is," Aelius says while walking, looking at the green fields.

"Et quam diversa a Romanis agris," Julius addit, ad agricultores laborantes in agris aspiciens.

"And how different from the Roman fields," Julius adds, watching the farmers working in the fields.

Subito, adiuvare agricolam carros trahentem vident. Carri gravati sunt et agricola laborat.

Suddenly, they see a farmer struggling to pull carts. The carts are heavy, and the farmer is working hard.

"Auxilium offeramus," Julius suadet, et ad agricolam accedunt.

"Let's offer help," Julius suggests, and they approach the farmer.

"Salve, agricola! Opus auxilio?" Aelius amice clamat.

"Hello, farmer! Do you need help?" Aelius calls out kindly.

"Ave, peregrini! Etiam, auxilium gratum est," agricola respondet, sudore madens.

"Greetings, travelers! Yes, help would be appreciated," the farmer replies, sweating heavily.

Ambo agricolam adiuvant, carros ad stabulum trahentes. Labor est durus, sed gaudent adiuvare.

Both help the farmer, pulling the carts to the stable. The work is hard, but they are glad to help.

Agricola, eis gratias agens, "Gratias vobis! Prandium vobis offertur pro labore vestro," dicit.

The farmer, thanking them, says, "Thank you! A meal is offered to you for your labor."

"Libenter accipimus," Julius respondet, et sub arbore prope agricolae casam prandent.

"We gladly accept," Julius replies, and they eat under a tree near the farmer's house.

Prandium est rusticum sed saporosum, panem et caseum et fructus continent. Sub arbore sedent, foliis autumni colore mutante.

The meal is simple but tasty, consisting of bread, cheese, and fruit. They sit under a tree, with autumn leaves changing color.

"Quam bene est hic esse, inter naturam," Aelius dicit, fructum edens.

"How good it is to be here, among nature," Aelius says, eating fruit.

"Vera dicis, Aelie. Rustica vita sua pulchritudine est," Julius consentit.

"You speak the truth, Aelius. The rustic life has its own beauty," Julius agrees.

Cum sol ad occasum vergit, iter suum pergunt. Ambulant sub caelo sereno, solis lumine aureo campos illuminante.

As the sun sets, they continue their journey. They walk under a clear sky, with the golden light of the sun illuminating the fields.

Ad vicum parvum perveniunt, ubi in parva casa pernoctant. Casa est simplicis structurae, sed calida et accogliens.

They arrive at a small village, where they spend the night in a small house. The house is of simple construction, but warm and welcoming.

"In hac casa, vita rustica sentitur," Julius dicit, in lecto recumbens.

"In this house, you can feel the rustic life," Julius says, lying down on the bed.

"Rusticorum vita dura est, sed honesta et plena tranquillitatis," Aelius addit, stellas per fenestram spectans.

"The life of farmers is hard, but honest and full of tranquility," Aelius adds, watching the stars through the window.

Dormiunt sub tecto casae, somniis pleni de agris et silvis et fluminibus Britanniae. Iter eorum ad Londinium prope est, sed etiam in hac parva vico, pulchritudinem et pacem vitae rusticae mirantur.

They sleep under the roof of the house, their dreams full of fields, forests, and rivers of Britain. Their journey to London is near, but even in this small village, they marvel at the beauty and peace of rustic life.

Capitulum IX: Prope Londinium

Aelius et Julius, post quietem in vico rustico, iter ad Londinium, finem itineris sui, pergunt. Sentire possunt Londinium iam prope esse.

Aelius and Julius, after resting in the rustic village, continue their journey to London, the end of their travels. They can feel that London is now near.

"Sentisne, Iuli? Londinium non longe est!" Aelius excitatus exclamat.

"Do you feel it, Julius? London is not far!" Aelius exclaims excitedly.

"Ita, Aelie. Post multos dies et multas periculas, tandem ad finem pervenimus," Julius respondet, cum spe in corde.

"Yes, Aelius. After many days and many dangers, we have finally reached the end," Julius responds, with hope in his heart.

Ambulant per vias lapideas, quae ad urbem ducunt. Vias et aedificationes Romanas, quae adhuc stant, admirantur.

They walk along the stone roads leading to the city. They admire the Roman roads and buildings that still stand.

"Vide, Aelie, quam mirae sunt hae aedificationes! Roma in Britannia," Julius dicit, aedificia antiqua spectans.

"Look, Aelius, how marvelous these buildings are! Rome in Britain," Julius says, gazing at the ancient structures.

"Romani vere ubique terrarum vestigia sua reliquerunt," Aelius addit, columnas et arcus spectans.

"The Romans truly left their mark all over the world," Aelius adds, looking at the columns and arches.

Subito, e latere viae, canis ferox apparet! Latrat et dentes ostendit, minax.

Suddenly, from the side of the road, a fierce dog appears! It barks and shows its teeth, threateningly.

"Protegamur!" Aelius clamat, et ambo fustes parvos tollunt, se a cane defendentes.

"Let's defend ourselves!" Aelius shouts, and both pick up small sticks, defending themselves from the dog.

Canis ad eos currit, sed Aelius et Julius eum fustibus repellunt, caute sed firmiter.

The dog runs toward them, but Aelius and Julius repel it with their sticks, cautiously but firmly.

E subito, incolae e proximis aedificiis exeunt et eos adiuvant. Canis ab incolis fugatur et tandem discedit.

Suddenly, the locals come out from nearby buildings and help them. The dog is chased away by the locals and finally leaves.

"Gratias vobis, boni homines!" Julius incolis dicit, anhelans.

"Thank you, good people!" Julius says to the locals, panting.

"Salvete, peregrini. Semper parati sumus adiuvare," incola respondet. "Cur huc venitis?"

"Greetings, travelers. We are always ready to help," a local responds. "Why have you come here?"

"Londinium iter facimus. Roma venimus," Aelius respondet.

"We are journeying to London. We come from Rome," Aelius responds.

"Londinium est urbs magna et pulchra. Multa ibi videre potestis," incola dicit, de urbe narrans.

"London is a great and beautiful city. There is much you can see there," the local says, telling them about the city.

Aelius et Julius incolis gratias agunt et de urbe Londinio plura discunt. Post colloquium, iter suum pergunt.

Aelius and Julius thank the locals and learn more about the city of London. After the conversation, they continue their journey.

Ad portas urbis appropinquant, magnas et firmas. Portae sunt testimonium potentiae et gloriae Londinii.

They approach the city's gates, large and strong. The gates are a testament to the power and glory of London.

"Ecce, portae urbis! Quam magnae et fortissimae!" Aelius dicit, portas spectans.

"Look, the city gates! How large and mighty!" Aelius says, gazing at the gates.

"Prope sumus, Aelie. Prope finem itineris nostri," Julius dicit, portas transiens.

"We are close, Aelius. Close to the end of our journey," Julius says, passing through the gates.

Et sic, Aelius et Julius, amici Romani, post multos dies et aventuras, ad Londinium, finem itineris longi et pleni periculis, perveniunt. Urbs ante eos iacet, plena historiae et vitae novae. Cor eorum spe et expectatione plenum est, quid futurum in hac urbe magna et incognita.

And so, Aelius and Julius, Roman friends, after many days and adventures, arrive in London, the end of their long and perilous journey. The city lies before them, full of history and new life. Their hearts are filled with hope and expectation, wondering what the future holds in this great and unknown city.

Capitulum X: Londinium

Aelius et Julius, post multas aventuras, tandem ad Londinium perveniunt. Urbs est magna et tumultuosa, viis latis plena hominum et curruum.

Aelius and Julius, after many adventures, finally arrive in London. The city is large and bustling, with wide streets full of people and carts.

"Incredibile!" Aelius exclamat, cum in urbem intrant. "Quam diversum est hoc a Roma nostra!"

"Incredible!" Aelius exclaims as they enter the city. "How different this is from our Rome!"

"Verum," Julius consentit. "Sed etiam similitudines sunt. Vide, viae stratae et aedificationes!"

"True," Julius agrees. "But there are also similarities. Look, paved roads and buildings!"

Ambulant per vias Londinii, hominum turbas et mercatores circumspicientes. Ad Forum Romanum, urbis cor, perveniunt.

They walk through the streets of London, observing the crowds of people and merchants. They arrive at the Roman Forum, the heart of the city.

"Forum Romanum! In corde Londinii!" Aelius dicit, ad forum spectans.

"The Roman Forum! In the heart of London!" Aelius says, looking at the forum.

In foro, multa sunt tabernacula et mercatores omnia vendentes. Aelius et Julius, commercium agunt, cibos et potiones emunt.

In the forum, there are many stalls and merchants selling all kinds of goods. Aelius and Julius do some shopping, buying food and drinks.

"Vide, Iuli, hae olivae et hic caseus!" Aelius dicit, emptiones delectatus.

"Look, Julius, these olives and this cheese!" Aelius says, delighted with his purchases.

"Et haec vina! Sicut in Italia," Julius addit, vinum odorans.

"And this wine! Just like in Italy," Julius adds, smelling the wine.

Postea, ad Thermae Romanae vadunt. Thermae sunt magnae et pulchrae, aqua calida et vaporibus plenae.

Afterwards, they go to the Roman Baths. The baths are large and beautiful, full of hot water and steam.

"Hic relaxari possumus post iter longum," Aelius dicit, in aquam calidam descendens.

"Here we can relax after a long journey," Aelius says, descending into the hot water.

"In thermis, fatigatio nostra alleviatur," Julius dicit, aqua fruens.

"In the baths, our fatigue is relieved," Julius says, enjoying the water.

Postquam in thermis relaxantur, ad amicum Aelii, qui in Londinio habitat, vadunt. Amicus eos laete accipit.

After relaxing in the baths, they go to Aelius's friend, who lives in London. The friend happily welcomes them.

"Aelie! Iuli! Salvete! Quam diu exspectavi vos!" amicus exclamat, eos amplexus.

"Aelius! Julius! Greetings! How long I have waited for you!" the friend exclaims, embracing them.

"Salve, amice! Tandem advenimus," Aelius respondet, amicum amplexans.

"Hello, friend! We have finally arrived," Aelius responds, embracing his friend.

In domo amici, cenam una edunt et de itinere suo narratur. Aelius et Julius, de periculis et aventuris suis per viam Romanam ad Londinium, fabulantur.

In their friend's house, they eat dinner together and tell the story of their journey. Aelius and Julius talk about the dangers and adventures they faced on the Roman road to London.

"Quae incredibilia narratis!" amicus dicit. "Vita vestra vere plena aventuris est."

"What incredible stories you tell!" the friend says. "Your life is truly full of adventures."

"Sed nunc, in Londinio, novam vitam incipiemus," Julius dicit, vinum in calice vertens.

"But now, in London, we will begin a new life," Julius says, swirling wine in his cup.

"In hac urbe, multa sunt facienda. Novas res discemus, novas personas conveniemus," Aelius addit, de futura vita cogitans.

"In this city, there is much to do. We will learn new things and meet new people," Aelius adds, thinking about the future.

Cena finita, de futuro colloquuntur. Londinium, plenum possibilitatum et aventurarum, eis novum domum erit.

After dinner, they talk about the future. London, full of possibilities and adventures, will be their new home.

"Gratias vobis pro hospitio, amice," Aelius dicit. "Cras, nova vita incipiet."

"Thank you for your hospitality, friend," Aelius says. "Tomorrow, a new life will begin."

"Et ego vobiscum ero, ut Londinium melius cognoscatis," amicus respondet.

"And I will be with you, so you can get to know London better," the friend replies.

Aelius et Julius, in Londinio, novam vitam incipiunt, plenam spei, periculis, et amicitiae.

Aelius and Julius, in London, begin a new life, full of hope, challenges, and friendship.

De Plauto, Comoediae Scriptore

Plautus fuit clarus scriptor Romanus. In Italia, in oppido Sarsina natus est. Natus est anno ducentesimo quinquagesimo quarto ante Christum natum. Multas fabulas Plautus scripsit.

Plautus was a famous Roman writer. He was born in Italy, in the town of Sarsina. He was born in the year 254 BC. Plautus wrote many plays.

Plautus comoedias Romanas composuit. Comoediae sunt fabulae risu plenae. Homines Romani fabulas Plauti amabant. In theatro, populus ridere et gaudere poterat.

Plautus composed Roman comedies. Comedies are plays full of laughter. The Roman people loved Plautus's plays. In the theater, the audience could laugh and enjoy themselves.

Fabulae Plauti de vita Romana narrabant. In fabulis, Plautus multos servos callidos, mercatores, milites, et deos descripsit. Servi in fabulis Plauti saepe callidi sunt et risum excitant.

Plautus's plays told stories about Roman life. In the plays, Plautus described many clever slaves, merchants, soldiers, and gods. The slaves in Plautus's plays are often clever and make the audience laugh.

Plautus linguam Latinam bene usus est. In fabulis, Plautus verba nova et iocos creavit. Stilus Plauti vivus et facilis est. Homines non solum in Roma sed etiam in toto orbe terrarum fabulas Plauti legunt.

Plautus used the Latin language well. In his plays, Plautus created new words and jokes. His style is lively and easy to follow. People not only in Rome but also around the world read Plautus's plays.

Plautus mortuus est anno centesimo octogesimo quarto ante Christum natum. Sed fabulae eius adhuc vivae sunt. Plautus est unus ex maximis scriptoribus Romanis. Opera eius adhuc studemus et in theatro spectamus.

Plautus died in the year 184 BC. But his plays are still alive. Plautus is one of the greatest Roman writers. We still study his works and watch them in the theater.

Plautus non solum comicus sed etiam magister vitae fuit. Per fabulas, Plautus de vita, amore, et humanitate nos docet. Comoediae eius adhuc risum et gaudium nobis praebent.

Plautus was not only a comedian but also a teacher of life. Through his plays, Plautus teaches us about life, love, and humanity. His comedies still bring us laughter and joy.

Et sic, Plautus, scriptor Romanus, in historia litterarum manet. Comoediae eius in memoria hominum semper erunt. Plautus nomen magnum in arte Romana et in litteris mundi tenet.

And so, Plautus, the Roman writer, remains in literary history. His comedies will always be in the memory of people. Plautus holds a great name in Roman art and in world literature.

Servus Astutus

Capitulum I: In Villa Patricii

In splendida villa Romana, Patricius, dives et nobilis Romanus, habitat. Domus eius magna est, ornamentis pulchris ornata.

In a splendid Roman villa, Patricius, a rich and noble Roman, lives. His house is large and decorated with beautiful ornaments.

Patricius filium habet, Marcum nomine, iuvenem Romanum, qui in amore est. Marcus est iuvenis fortis et pulcher, sed timidus in amore.

Patricius has a son, named Marcus, a young Roman who is in love. Marcus is a strong and handsome young man, but shy in matters of love.

In domo etiam est servus, Stichus nomine. Stichus est servus astutus et fidelis, semper paratus ad dominum suum adiuvandum.

In the house, there is also a servant named Stichus. Stichus is a clever and loyal servant, always ready to help his master.

Quadam die, Patricius Marcum in atrium vocat. Marcus ad patrem suum venit, paratus ad audiendum.

One day, Patricius calls Marcus to the atrium. Marcus comes to his father, ready to listen.

"Marcum, fili mi," Patricius serio dicit. "Tempus est tibi uxorem ducere. Familia nostra hoc exspectat."

"Marcus, my son," Patricius says seriously. "It is time for you to marry. Our family expects this."

Marcus, cogitans, respondet: "Pater, amor meus est puella nomine Lydia. Illa vicina nostra est, pulchra et docta."

Marcus, thinking, replies: "Father, my love is a girl named Lydia. She is our neighbor, beautiful and learned."

"Lydia, eh?" Patricius miratus dicit. "Sed, fili, numquid illa scit te amare?"

"Lydia, eh?" Patricius says, surprised. "But, son, does she know that you love her?"

"Minime, pater. Ego sum nimis timidus," Marcus confitetur, caput demittens.

"No, father. I am too shy," Marcus confesses, lowering his head.

Stichus, qui prope stat et omnia audit, ad Marcum accedit. "Domine, fortasse possum tibi auxilium dare in amore."

Stichus, who is standing nearby and hears everything, approaches Marcus. "Master, perhaps I can help you in love."

"Stiche, servus fidelis es, quid autem facere potes?" Marcus curiose interrogat.

"Stichus, you are a faithful servant, but what can you do?" Marcus asks curiously.

"Domine, mihi consilium est," Stichus dicit. "Promitto tibi, Lydiam tecum colloqui faciam. Astutia mea utar."

"Master, I have a plan," Stichus says. "I promise you, I will make Lydia speak with you. I will use my cunning."

Marcus, spe repleta, "Stiche, si hoc facis, magnas gratias tibi habeo. Me adiuvare potes?"

Marcus, filled with hope, says, "Stichus, if you do this, I will be very grateful to you. Can you help me?"

"Certe, domine. Modo mihi fides et omnia bene evenient," Stichus confirmat, consilium iam in mente formans.

"Certainly, master. Just trust me, and everything will go well," Stichus assures him, already forming a plan in his mind.

Et sic incipit fabula, cum Stichus, servus astutus, consilium capit ut dominum suum in amore adiuvet.

And so the story begins, with Stichus, the clever servant, devising a plan to help his master in love.

Capitulum II: Consilium Astutum

Stichus, servus astutus, consilium capit et ad villam Lydiae, puellae quam Marcus amat, festinanter it. Viae Romae sunt plenae hominum et curruum, sed Stichus non tardatur.

Stichus, the clever servant, makes a plan and hurries to the villa of Lydia, the girl whom Marcus loves. The streets of Rome are full of people and carts, but Stichus is not delayed.

Ad villam perveniens, Deliam, ancillam Lydiae, in horto invenit. Delia est ancilla iuvenis et vivax, Lydiae fideliter servit.

Upon arriving at the villa, he finds Delia, Lydia's maid, in the garden. Delia is a young and lively servant, faithfully serving Lydia.

"Salve, Delia! Ego Stichus sum, servus domini Marci. Habemus consilium pro domina tua," Stichus salutans dicit.

"Hello, Delia! I am Stichus, servant of Marcus. We have a plan for your mistress," Stichus says, greeting her.

Delia, subridens, "Salve, Stiche! Quid est hoc consilium? Curate audire volo," respondet.

Delia, smiling, responds, "Hello, Stichus! What is this plan? I'm eager to hear it."

Stichus, circumspiciens ne quis audiat, ad Deliam appropinquat. "Domina tua, Lydia, a domino meo Marco amatur. Marcus autem nimis timidus est ut suum amorem Lydiae confiteatur."

Stichus, looking around to make sure no one hears, approaches Delia. "Your mistress, Lydia, is loved by my master Marcus. However, Marcus is too shy to confess his love to Lydia."

Delia risum vix continet. "Vere? Dominus tuus nostram dominam amat? Haec res ridicula et dulcis est!"

Delia can hardly contain her laughter. "Really? Your master loves our mistress? This is both amusing and sweet!"

Stichus, "Sic est. Sed opus est auxilio tuo. Visne nobis in hoc consilio adiuvare?" rogat.

Stichus replies, "Indeed. But we need your help. Will you assist us in this plan?"

Delia, caput inclinans, "Ego Lydiae fidem habeo. Narrabo ei. Fortasse dominam meam hoc consilium placet. Sed quid exacte facere debemus?"

Delia, nodding her head, says, "I am loyal to Lydia. I will tell her. Perhaps my mistress will like this plan. But what exactly should we do?"

Stichus, "Tu dominae tuae de amore Marci narra. Ego Marcum adiuvabo ut se magis confidentem praestet. Forsitan in horto aut in via Lydiae Marcum 'casu' inveniat."

Stichus replies, "You tell your mistress about Marcus's love. I will help Marcus appear more confident. Perhaps Marcus will 'accidentally' meet Lydia in the garden or on the street."

Delia, consilium probans, "Bene, Stiche. Ego dominae meae narrabo. Tu Marci nuntia ut paratus sit."

Delia, approving of the plan, says, "Good, Stichus. I will tell my mistress. You inform Marcus so that he can be ready."

Stichus et Delia, consilium ridentes coniurant, et Stichus ad Marcum redit ut nuntium bonum ferat.

Stichus and Delia, laughing, conspire on the plan, and Stichus returns to Marcus to bring the good news.

Ad Marcum reversus, "Domine, consilium inceptum est. Delia dominae suae de te narrabit," Stichus laetans dicit.

Returning to Marcus, Stichus says joyfully, "Master, the plan is in motion. Delia will tell her mistress about you."

Marcus, audito hoc, vultu laeto et spe repleto, "Stiche, si hoc verum fit, maximas tibi gratias habeam! Amor meus fortasse tandem fructum feret!"

Marcus, upon hearing this, with a happy and hopeful expression, says, "Stichus, if this comes true, I will be deeply grateful to you! Perhaps my love will finally bear fruit!"

Et sic, consilium astutum incipit moveri, spes in corde Marci augens. Sed num Lydia, pulchra et docta puella, hunc amorem respondebit? Futurum incertum est, sed amor, ut dicitur, omnia vincit.

And so, the clever plan begins to unfold, with hope growing in Marcus's heart. But will Lydia, the beautiful and learned girl, return this love? The future is uncertain, but as they say, love conquers all.

Capitulum III: Paratus ad Colloquium

In villa patricii, Marcus, filius Patricii, paratus est ad colloquium cum Lydia. Vestimenta optima induit, speculum inspiciens.

In the villa of the nobleman, Marcus, the son of Patricius, is ready for a conversation with Lydia. He wears his best clothes, looking into the mirror.

Stichus, servus fidelis, ad Marcum accedit. "Domine, memento ut suavis et urbanus sis. Lydia pulchra et docta est; eam delectare debes."

Stichus, the faithful servant, approaches Marcus. "Master, remember to be charming and polite. Lydia is beautiful and learned; you must please her."

Lydia et Delia, sub sole matutino, ad villam Marci veniunt. Lydia est puella pulchra, oculis claris et risu suavi.

Lydia and Delia, under the morning sun, come to Marcus's villa. Lydia is a beautiful girl, with bright eyes and a sweet smile.

Marcus, Lydiae appropinquante, valde nervosus fit. "Salve, Lydia," tremula voce dicit, manum eius suaviter tenens.

Marcus, as Lydia approaches, becomes very nervous. "Hello, Lydia," he says in a trembling voice, gently holding her hand.

Lydia, Marci salutatione delectata, subridet. "Salve, Marcus. Quam elegans es hodie!" ait, eum laudans.

Lydia, pleased by Marcus's greeting, smiles. "Hello, Marcus. How elegant you are today!" she says, praising him.

Stichus et Delia, prope stantes, subridendo se abscondunt, consilium suum feliciter procedere videntes.

Stichus and Delia, standing nearby, hide their smiles, seeing that their plan is progressing successfully.

Marcus et Lydia in hortum ambulant, de musicis Romanis et libris popularibus loquentes. Sol altus in caelo est, et aves canunt.

Marcus and Lydia walk into the garden, talking about Roman music and popular books. The sun is high in the sky, and the birds are singing.

"Forte, Lydia, librum 'De Amore' legis?" Marcus interrogat, florem pulchrum carpens et ei dant.

"By chance, Lydia, do you read the book 'On Love'?" Marcus asks, picking a beautiful flower and giving it to her.

"Etiam, 'De Amore' legi. Librum amo!" Lydia respondet, florem accipiens. "Tu quoque, Marcus, libris delectaris?"

"Yes, I have read 'On Love.' I love the book!" Lydia responds, accepting the flower. "Do you also enjoy books, Marcus?"

"Vero," Marcus ait. "Libri et musica vitam meam laetam faciunt."

"Truly," Marcus says. "Books and music make my life happy."

Dum ambulant, amor inter eos sensim crescit. Fabulantur de rebus variis, risus et verba suavia inter se partientes.

As they walk, love slowly grows between them. They talk about various topics, sharing laughter and sweet words.

Post longam et iucundam conversationem, Marcus audacter rogat: "Lydia, visne mecum cenare hodie vespere?"

After a long and pleasant conversation, Marcus boldly asks, "Lydia, would you like to have dinner with me this evening?"

Lydia, paulum rubescens, "Marcus, libenter tecum cenabo," respondet.

Lydia, blushing slightly, responds, "Marcus, I would be happy to have dinner with you."

Et sic, Marcus et Lydia, inter risus et colloquia suavia, diem agunt. Amor inter eos, ut videtur, pulchre floret. Stichus et Delia, consilium suum prosperum videntes, in angulo se celant, gaudentes et sperantes in futurum felix.

And so, Marcus and Lydia spend the day between laughter and sweet conversations. The love between them, it seems, is beautifully blossoming. Stichus and Delia, seeing their plan succeed, hide in a corner, rejoicing and hoping for a happy future.

Capitulum IV: Cena Iucunda

Serena vespera, in horto patricii, cena romantica paratur. Lydia, pulchra Romana puella, cenam cum Marco, filio Patricii, accipit.

On a calm evening, a romantic dinner is prepared in the nobleman's garden. Lydia, a beautiful Roman girl, shares dinner with Marcus, the son of Patricius.

Hortus villae magnifice ornatus est. Lumina leniter lucent, et flores ubique positi sunt, suaves odores spargentes.

The villa's garden is magnificently decorated. Lights gently glow, and flowers are placed everywhere, spreading sweet fragrances.

Stichus, servus astutus et coquus peritus, cenam optimam coquit. Ex coquina odores delectabiles veniunt, epulas exquisitas promittentes.

Stichus, the clever servant and skilled cook, prepares an excellent meal. From the kitchen come delightful smells, promising exquisite dishes.

Marcus et Lydia ad mensam eleganter paratam sedent. Marcus, ornatus et sollicitus, Lydiae locum offert.

Marcus and Lydia sit at the elegantly prepared table. Marcus, well-dressed and a bit nervous, offers Lydia her seat.

Vinum rubrum in pocula infundunt et bibunt. "De astris nocturnis loquamur," Marcus proponit, ad caelum spectans.

Red wine is poured into their cups, and they drink. "Let's talk about the night stars," Marcus suggests, looking up at the sky.

Lydia, vinum gustans, "Stellae noctu tam pulchrae sunt," ait. "Stella tua quae est?"

Lydia, tasting the wine, says, "The stars at night are so beautiful. Which star is your favorite?"

"Sic est," Marcus assentitur. "Mihi, Venus, stella amoris, est favorita."

"Indeed," Marcus agrees. "For me, Venus, the star of love, is my favorite."

Inter risus et colloquia dulcia, cena procedit. Cibus exquisitus est, et vinum laetitiam affert.

Amid laughter and sweet conversations, the dinner progresses. The food is exquisite, and the wine brings joy.

Marcus, momento opportuno captato, Lydiam intente aspicit. "Lydia, tecum semper esse volo," serio et amore pleno dicit.

Marcus, seizing the right moment, looks intently at Lydia. "Lydia, I want to always be with you," he says seriously and full of love.

Lydia, audito hoc, rubore suffusa, "Marcus, et ego...," incipit, sed verba in gaudii sensu desinunt.

Lydia, blushing upon hearing this, begins, "Marcus, I also...," but her words trail off in a feeling of joy.

E longinquo, Stichus et Delia, qui omnia paraverunt, spectant. Vident dominum suum et Lydiam felices, et ipsi laetantur.

From a distance, Stichus and Delia, who prepared everything, watch. They see their master and Lydia happy, and they rejoice.

"Credo dominum nostrum amorem verum invenisse," Delia susurrat.

"I believe our master has found true love," Delia whispers.

"Et ego," Stichus addit. "Consilium nostrum feliciter cessit."

"And I," Stichus adds. "Our plan has succeeded beautifully."

Luna in caelo alto lucet, et stellae micant. In horto patricii, amor inter Marcum et Lydiam floret, et nox est magica et romantica. Stichus et Delia, in umbra stantes, sperant futurum esse felix pro domino suo et domina amata.

The moon shines high in the sky, and the stars twinkle. In the nobleman's garden, the love between Marcus and Lydia blossoms, and the night is magical and romantic. Stichus and Delia, standing in the shadows, hope for a happy future for their master and his beloved lady.

Capitulum V: Invidia Patricii

Post cenam iucundam, nuntius ad Patricium, patrem Marci, de eventu pervenit. Patricius, audito filio suo cum Lydia sine suo consilio cenasse, iratus est.

After the pleasant dinner, news reached Patricius, Marcus's father, about the event. Patricius, upon hearing that his son had dined with Lydia without his counsel, was angry.

"Quid hoc est? Filius meus sine mea scientia et consilio cum puella cenat!" Patricius in atrio villae clamat, fronte contracta.

"What is this? My son dines with a girl without my knowledge or advice!" Patricius shouts in the villa's atrium, his brow furrowed.

Stichus, qui semper astutus et fidelis est, ad Patricium accedit, eum placare conatus. "Domine, quaeso, me audi. Amor inter Marcum et Lydiam est, non insania. Nonne amor est maximus in vita?"

Stichus, who is always clever and loyal, approaches Patricius, trying to calm him. "Master, please listen to me. The love between Marcus and Lydia is not madness. Isn't love the greatest thing in life?"

Patricius, verbis Stichi auditis, paulatim movetur. Amor filii sui in mente eius resonat. "Forsitan recte dicis, Stiche. Sed difficile est mihi hoc accipere."

Patricius, after hearing Stichus's words, is gradually moved. His son's love echoes in his mind. "Perhaps you are right, Stichus. But it is hard for me to accept this."

"Bene, videamus si haec Lydia digna est filio meo," Patricius post paulum dicit, cogitationibus suis victus.

"Well, let's see if this Lydia is worthy of my son," Patricius says after a moment, overcome by his thoughts.

Marcus, cum Patricius eum vocat, timet sed sperat. "Pater, Lydia puella est pulchra et docta. Digna est nostro amore et honore."

When Patricius calls Marcus, he is afraid but hopeful. "Father, Lydia is a beautiful and learned girl. She is worthy of our love and honor."

"Videbimus," Patricius respondet. "Eam ad cenam in nostra villa invita. Ego ipsam iudicabo."

"We will see," Patricius responds. "Invite her to dinner at our villa. I will judge her myself."

Marcus, spe plenus, ad Lydiam nuntium mittit. Lydia, nuntio accepto, ad villam Patricii venit, ornata et elegans.

Marcus, full of hope, sends a message to Lydia. Lydia, after receiving the message, comes to Patricius's villa, dressed beautifully and elegantly.

Cum Lydia advenit, Patricius eam intente inspicit. "Salve, Lydia. Multa de te audivi," dicit, vocem suam celans.

When Lydia arrives, Patricius inspects her intently. "Hello, Lydia. I have heard much about you," he says, hiding his tone.

"Salve, domine Patricii. Gratum est me hic invitari," Lydia respondet, voce suavi et composita.

"Hello, Lord Patricius. I am grateful to be invited here," Lydia responds, with a sweet and composed voice.

Cenam, Patricius, Marcus, et Lydia una edunt. Patricius Lydiam probat, eius eruditionem et elegantiam admirans.

Patricius, Marcus, and Lydia eat dinner together. Patricius approves of Lydia, admiring her knowledge and elegance.

"Lydia, intellego nunc cur filius meus te tam magni aestimet. Es docta et grata puella," Patricius tandem dicit, cor suum amori filii sui aperiens.

"Lydia, I now understand why my son holds you in such high regard. You are a learned and graceful girl," Patricius finally says, opening his heart to his son's love.

Marcus et Lydia, verbis his auditis, gaudent et se invicem aspiciunt, amor in oculis eorum lucentibus. Stichus et Delia, e longinquo spectantes, sibi congratulantur subridendo. Amor vincit omnia, etiam patris invidiam.

Marcus and Lydia, hearing these words, rejoice and look at each other, love shining in their eyes. Stichus and Delia, watching from afar, smile and congratulate themselves. Love conquers all, even a father's jealousy.

Capitulum VI: Obstaculum Novum

In fabula nostra, novum obstaculum apparet. Lydiae pater, Senex nomine, dives et severus, in urbem Romanam venit. Fama de amore Lydiae et Marci ad eum pervenit, et non vult filiam suam nubere iuveni Romano.

In our story, a new obstacle appears. Lydia's father, called Senex, a rich and stern man, comes to the city of Rome. News of Lydia and Marcus's love has reached him, and he does not want his daughter to marry a young Roman.

Senex, in villam Patricii veniens, "Lydia, filia mea, non nubet Marco. Ego alium virum dignum tibi inveniam!" severo tono dicit.

Senex, arriving at Patricius's villa, says in a stern tone, "Lydia, my daughter, will not marry Marcus. I will find you another worthy man!"

Marcus et Lydia, hoc audientes, tristes et solliciti fiunt. Amor eorum subito minari sentiunt, spes eorum in periculo est.

Marcus and Lydia, hearing this, become sad and worried. They suddenly feel their love is threatened, and their hopes are in danger.

"Marco, pater meus durus est et severus. Sed te amo, et cor meum tibi deditum est," Lydia lacrimans ad Marcum dicit.

"Marcus, my father is harsh and strict. But I love you, and my heart is devoted to you," Lydia says to Marcus, crying.

Stichus, servus fidelis et astutus, consilium novum capit. "Domine Marcus, domina Lydia, fidem habete! Inveniam viam ut cor Senecis molliatur," Stichus confidens dicit.

Stichus, the faithful and clever servant, comes up with a new plan. "Master Marcus, Lady Lydia, have faith! I will find a way to soften Senex's heart," Stichus says confidently.

Stichus, callidus, Senecem ad cenam in villa Patricii invitat. "Domine Senex, honorem nobis facias si ad cenam nostram venias," Stichus dicit.

Cunning Stichus invites Senex to dinner at Patricius's villa. "Lord Senex, it would be an honor if you came to our dinner," Stichus says.

Senex, curiositate motus, invitationem accipit. "Videbimus quid isti Romani possint," inquit, ad villam veniens.

Senex, moved by curiosity, accepts the invitation. "We'll see what these Romans can do," he says, arriving at the villa.

In cena, Stichus vinum eximium, quod hilaritatem et bonum animum movet, Seneci dat. "Domine Senex, hoc vinum te delectabit," Stichus dicit, poculum plenum offerens.

At dinner, Stichus gives Senex an excellent wine, which brings joy and good spirits. "Lord Senex, this wine will delight you," Stichus says, offering a full cup.

Senex, vino affectus, sensim hilaris fit. Risus eius, qui rarus est, in villa resonat. "Haha, haec Romana hospitalitas est iucunda!" exclamat.

Affected by the wine, Senex gradually becomes cheerful. His laughter, which is rare, echoes through the villa. "Haha, this Roman hospitality is delightful!" he exclaims.

Marcus et Lydia, hoc videntes, sibi invicem subridendo sperant. "Forsitan pater meus sententiam mutabit," Lydia susurrat.

Marcus and Lydia, seeing this, smile at each other with hope. "Perhaps my father will change his mind," Lydia whispers.

Stichus et Delia, e longinquo spectantes, gaudent vino suo effectum facere. "Bene facis, Stiche. Fortasse amor vincet," Delia dicit.

Stichus and Delia, watching from a distance, are pleased to see the wine taking effect. "Well done, Stichus. Perhaps love will win," Delia says.

Cena finita, Senex, vino et hospitalitate delectatus, magis apertus et laetus videtur. "Romani non sunt tam mali quam putabam," inquit, ridens.

After the dinner, Senex, delighted by the wine and hospitality, seems more open and happy. "The Romans are not as bad as I thought," he says, laughing.

Marcus et Lydia, hoc audientes, magis sperant. Fortasse amor eorum viam inveniet, etiam in corde patris severi. Stichus, servus astutus, ridet, consilium suum procedere videns.

Marcus and Lydia, hearing this, feel even more hopeful. Perhaps their love will find a way, even in the heart of a strict father. Stichus, the clever servant, smiles, seeing his plan progressing.

Capitulum VII: Senex Mollitur

In sequenti capitulo fabulae nostrae, Senex, Lydiae pater, vino hilaris, in villa Patricii ad cenam sedet. Lumina suaviter lumen dant, et omnes laetitia fruuntur.

In the next chapter of our story, Senex, Lydia's father, sits happily at dinner in Patricius's villa, cheered by wine. The lights softly glow, and everyone enjoys the happiness.

Senex, vino commotus, fabulam de iuventute sua narrat. "Cum iuvenis essem, et ego amore ardebam," inquit, magno cum risu. "Vita plena est miris eventibus."

Moved by the wine, Senex tells a story about his youth. "When I was young, I too burned with love," he says with a great laugh. "Life is full of wonderful events."

Stichus, qui semper est astutus, opportunitatem capit. "Domine Senex, cum de amore dicimus, amor Marci et Lydiae magni ponderis est," caute dicit.

Stichus, who is always clever, seizes the opportunity. "Lord Senex, when we speak of love, the love between Marcus and Lydia is of great importance," he says cautiously.

Senex, adhuc vino hilaris, verbis Stichi audit et ponderat. "Hmm," inquit, "iuvenes saepe amant. Forsitan iuvenes suam viam invenire debent."

Senex, still cheerful from the wine, listens to Stichus's words and thinks. "Hmm," he says, "young people often love. Perhaps they must find their own way."

Post cenam, Senex in horto solus ambulat, amore Marci et Lydiae meditans. Luna in caelo clare lucet, et stellae scintillant. "Forsitan amor verus est," susurrat.

After dinner, Senex walks alone in the garden, thinking about Marcus and Lydia's love. The moon shines brightly in the sky, and the stars twinkle. "Perhaps love is true," he whispers.

Marcus et Lydia, hoc audientes, novam spem concipiunt. Senex, qui semper durus et severus videbatur, nunc cor mollit. Amor eorum fortasse viam inveniet.

Marcus and Lydia, hearing this, feel a new hope. Senex, who always seemed harsh and strict, now softens his heart. Perhaps their love will find a way.

Stichus et Delia, e longinquo spectantes, consilium suum prosperum esse gaudent. "Videtur dominus Senex mollescere," Delia dicit.

Stichus and Delia, watching from afar, are pleased that their plan is succeeding. "It seems Lord Senex is softening," Delia says.

"Amor vincit omnia," Stichus subridet et respondet. "Fiduciam habemus in amore Marci et Lydiae."

"Love conquers all," Stichus smiles and replies. "We have faith in the love between Marcus and Lydia."

Senex, post multam meditationem, ad Marcum et Lydiam accedit. "Iuvenes," inquit, "multum cogitavi. Forsitan errem vos in amore vestro impedire."

After much thought, Senex approaches Marcus and Lydia. "Young ones," he says, "I have thought a lot. Perhaps I am wrong to hinder your love."

Marcus et Lydia, his verbis auditis, vix sibi credunt. Eorum gaudium immensum est. "Pater, tibi gratias agimus," Lydia cum lacrimis gaudii dicit.

Marcus and Lydia, hearing these words, can hardly believe it. Their joy is immense. "Father, we thank you," Lydia says with tears of joy.

Senex, ad filiam suam respiciens, ait, "Lydia, semper te dilexi. Si Marcus te beatam facit, ego consentio."

Senex, looking at his daughter, says, "Lydia, I have always loved you. If Marcus makes you happy, I give my consent."

Et sic, in villa Patricii, amor triumphat. Senex, olim durus, nunc animo demollito, amorem filiae suae et Marci approbat. Stichus et Delia, in angulo celati, inter se congratulantur. Amor, ut apparet, omnia superat.

And so, in Patricius's villa, love triumphs. Senex, once harsh, now with a softened heart, approves of the love between his daughter and Marcus. Stichus and Delia, hidden in a corner, congratulate each other. Love, it seems, conquers all.

Capitulum VIII: Consensus et Gaudium

Senex postquam adsensit, magnum gaudium in villa Patricii ortum est. Omnes gaudent, et festum nuptiale mox paratur.

After Senex gave his consent, great joy arose in Patricius's villa. Everyone rejoices, and the wedding celebration is soon prepared.

Senex Marcum et Lydiam ad villam suam grandem et pulchram invitat. "Lydia, filia mea, tibi licet Marcum ducere. Benedictiones meas vobis do," Senex, Lydiae pater, sollemniter inquit. In atrio villae, cum manibus iunctis, Senex benedictionem pronuntiat.

Senex invites Marcus and Lydia to his large and beautiful villa. "Lydia, my daughter, you are allowed to marry Marcus. I give you both my blessings," Senex, Lydia's father, solemnly says. In the villa's atrium, with hands joined, Senex pronounces the blessing.

Marcus et Lydia, verbis Senecis auditis, maximo gaudio afficiuntur et sese amplexantur. Amor eorum nunc firmior quam umquam antea videtur. "Gratias tibi, pater," Lydia lacrimis laetis inquit. Marcus, manum eius tenens, "Gratias tibi, domine Senex. Promitto, Lydia semper in amore et cura erit," respondet.

Marcus and Lydia, upon hearing Senex's words, are filled with great joy and embrace each other. Their love now seems stronger than ever before. "Thank you, father," Lydia says with joyful tears. Marcus, holding her hand, responds, "Thank you, Lord Senex. I promise, Lydia will always be cared for and loved."

Patricius, pater Marci, et Senex, de futuro filiorum suorum colloquuntur. "Filius meus et filia tua felices erunt. Hoc certum est," Patricius inquit. Senex, nunc lenior et serenus, "Spero. Amor iuvenum saepe sapientior est quam cogitamus," respondet.

Patricius, Marcus's father, and Senex talk about their children's future. "My son and your daughter will be happy. This is certain," Patricius says. Senex, now softer and calm, replies, "I hope so. Young love is often wiser than we think."

Stichus et Delia, qui consilium amoris texuerunt, in angulo stantes, gaudent. "Vidisti, Delia? Amor vincit omnia," Stichus subridens inquit. "Etiam, Stiche. Domini nostri nunc in amore et felicitate sunt," Delia cum gaudio respondet.

Stichus and Delia, who wove the plan of love, stand in the corner, rejoicing. "Did you see, Delia? Love conquers all," Stichus says with a smile. "Yes, Stichus. Our masters are now in love and happiness," Delia replies with joy.

In villa, ubi festum nuptiale celebratur, amici et familiares conveniunt. Musica dulcis auditur, cantus et risus per auras volitant. Saltatio et hilaritas in hortis et atrio repletur.

In the villa, where the wedding feast is celebrated, friends and family gather. Sweet music is heard, and songs and laughter float through the air. Dancing and joy fill the gardens and the atrium.

Marcus et Lydia, in medio horti, in vinculo amoris, circumdantur ab amicis et familia. "Amor et fortuna nobiscum sunt," Marcus ad Lydiam inquit, in oculos eius intuens. "Et semper erunt," Lydia respondet, manum eius stringens.

Marcus and Lydia, in the middle of the garden, bound by love, are surrounded by friends and family. "Love and fortune are with us," Marcus says to Lydia, gazing into her eyes. "And they always will be," Lydia replies, squeezing his hand.

Nox progreditur, et stellae in caelo micant super festum plenum amoris et gaudii. In villa Patricii, novum capitulum in vita Marci et Lydiae incipit, plenum spe, amore, et felicitate. Stichus et Delia, e longinquo spectantes, sibi subridendo, scire se partem huius fabulae felicis.

The night progresses, and the stars twinkle in the sky above the feast full of love and joy. In Patricius's villa, a new chapter in Marcus and Lydia's life begins, full of hope, love, and happiness. Stichus and Delia, watching from afar, smile at each other, knowing they are part of this happy story.

Capitulum IX: Nuptiae Celebrantur

In fabula "Servus Astutus," dies magnus nuptiarum adventus est. Villa Patricii festivitate repletur, et omnes ad magnam celebrationem parati sunt.

In the story "The Clever Servant," the great day of the wedding has arrived. Patricius's villa is filled with festivity, and everyone is ready for the grand celebration.

Lydia, futura sponsa, in veste nuptiali candida et splendida, pulcherrima apparet. Ornamenta eius splendent, et omnium oculi in eam defixi sunt. "Quam pulchra es, Lydia!" amicae eius exclamant, eam circumdantes.

Lydia, the future bride, appears most beautiful in her bright, shining wedding dress. Her ornaments sparkle, and all eyes are fixed on her. "How beautiful you are, Lydia!" her friends exclaim, surrounding her.

Marcus, sponsus, ante altare stat, cor plenum nervis sed etiam laetitia. Cum Lydia ad altare graditur, eius pulchritudo eum afficit. "Lydia, mea futura uxor," susurrat, eam admirans.

Marcus, the groom, stands before the altar, his heart full of nerves but also joy. As Lydia walks towards the altar, her beauty overwhelms him. "Lydia, my future wife," he whispers, admiring her.

Sacerdos Romanus, togatus et sollemnis, ad altare accedit et ceremoniam nuptialem incipit. "Hodie, duo corda in unum iunguntur," sacerdos voce clara pronuntiat.

The Roman priest, dressed in a toga and solemn, approaches the altar and begins the wedding ceremony. "Today, two hearts are joined as one," the priest proclaims in a clear voice.

"In matrimonium vos iungo," sacerdos proclamat, manum super capita Marci et Lydiae tenens. Omnes in silentio audiunt, momenti magnitudinem percipientes.

"I join you in marriage," the priest proclaims, holding his hand over Marcus and Lydia's heads. Everyone listens in silence, sensing the significance of the moment.

Anuli nuptiales, signa amoris et fidelitatis, inter Marcum et Lydiam traduntur. Marcus anulum in digitum Lydiae ponit, et Lydia similiter facit. "In aeternum," uterque subridens inquit.

The wedding rings, symbols of love and loyalty, are exchanged between Marcus and Lydia. Marcus places the ring on Lydia's finger, and Lydia does the same. "Forever," each says with a smile.

Postquam anuli dati sunt, Marcus et Lydia osculum nuptiale dant. Populus, amoris eorum testis, plaudit et laetatur. "Vivat sponsus et sponsa!" clamant.

After the rings are given, Marcus and Lydia share their wedding kiss. The crowd, witnessing their love, applauds and celebrates. "Long live the bride and groom!" they shout.

Convivium magnum in villa incipit. Est edulia lautissima et vinum lectissimum ubique. Tabulae largae convivas excipiunt, risus et sermones per auras volitantes.

A grand feast begins in the villa. There is the finest food and the choicest wine everywhere. Large tables welcome the guests, with laughter and conversations filling the air.

Inter convivas, Stichus et Delia saltant et ridunt, gaudentes in successu consilii sui. "Vidisti, Delia? Omnia prospere eveniunt!" Stichus exclamat, manu eius in saltatione ducente.

Among the guests, Stichus and Delia dance and laugh, rejoicing in the success of their plan. "Did you see, Delia? Everything is turning out perfectly!" Stichus exclaims, leading her in the dance.

"Felicem diem vidi," Stichus ad Deliam inquit, cum vinum bibunt. "Amor Marci et Lydiae nunc celebratur, et nos pars huius historiae sumus."

"I've seen a happy day," Stichus says to Delia, as they drink wine. "The love of Marcus and Lydia is now being celebrated, and we are part of this story."

Delia, oculos in Stichum figens, "Stiche, nobis quoque fortasse amor in futuro est," ridens inquit. Stichus, hoc audito, rubet sed subridet.

Delia, fixing her eyes on Stichus, says with a smile, "Stichus, perhaps love is in our future as well." Stichus, hearing this, blushes but smiles.

Nox procedit, et festum plenum est musica, risu, et gaudio. Marcus et Lydia, nunc maritus et uxor, in medio convivii sunt, manibus iunctis, oculis in futurum plenos spe et amore directi.

The night goes on, and the feast is full of music, laughter, and joy. Marcus and Lydia, now husband and wife, stand in the middle of the celebration, holding hands, their eyes filled with hope and love for the future.

In villa Patricii, amor vincit, et nuptiae Marci et Lydiae diem memorabilem in vita omnium efficiunt. Stichus et Delia, cum ceteris, in festivitate noctis partem habent, felices et contenti.

In Patricius's villa, love triumphs, and the wedding of Marcus and Lydia makes a memorable day in the lives of everyone. Stichus and Delia, along with the others, take part in the night's festivities, happy and content.

Capitulum X: Vita Nova

Post nuptias magnificas, Marcus et Lydia in villa nova, pulchra et tranquilla, habitant. Domus eorum est plena amoris et laetitiae.

After the magnificent wedding, Marcus and Lydia live in a new, beautiful, and peaceful villa. Their home is full of love and joy.

Amor inter Marcum et Lydiam cotidie crescit. Omnes dies sunt pleni risu, colloquiis dulcibus, et momentis felicibus. "Nunquam credidi me tam felicem esse posse," Marcus ad Lydiam dicit, eam amplexans.

The love between Marcus and Lydia grows every day. Each day is full of laughter, sweet conversations, and happy moments. "I never thought I could be this happy," Marcus says to Lydia, embracing her.

Stichus, servus fidelis et astutus, adhuc apud eos manet, nunc non solum servus sed etiam amicus et consiliarius. "Domine Marcus, domina Lydia, semper ad vestrum servitium," Stichus dicit, semper paratus ad adiuvandum.

Stichus, the loyal and clever servant, still remains with them, now not just a servant but also a friend and advisor. "Master Marcus, Lady Lydia, always at your service," Stichus says, always ready to help.

Delia quoque cum Lydia manet, non solum ut ancilla sed etiam ut amica fida. "Domina Lydia, semper tecum ero," Delia dicit, Lydiam in consiliis et cotidianis rebus adiuvans.

Delia also stays with Lydia, not only as a maid but also as a loyal friend. "Lady Lydia, I will always be with you," Delia says, helping Lydia with advice and daily tasks.

Patricius, pater Marci, et Senex, pater Lydiae, eos saepe visitant. Vident filios suos felices esse et gaudent. "Vita vestra exemplar amoris est," Patricius ad eos dicit.

Patricius, Marcus's father, and Senex, Lydia's father, often visit them. They see that their children are happy and rejoice. "Your life is an example of love," Patricius says to them.

Marcus, in horto ambulans, "Vita nostra gaudio plena est. Te habens, Lydia, nihil deest," inquit. Lydia, docta et felix, Marcum amat et verba eius corde suo accipit.

Marcus, walking in the garden, says, "Our life is full of joy. Having you, Lydia, nothing is lacking." Lydia, wise and happy, loves Marcus and receives his words in her heart.

Stichus et Delia, qui totam historiam amoris viderunt, in angulo stantes, subridendo spectant. "Vidisti, Delia? Amor omnia potest," Stichus ad Deliam inquit, manum eius tenens.

Stichus and Delia, who have witnessed the whole love story, stand in the corner, smiling as they watch. "Did you see, Delia? Love can do anything," Stichus says to Delia, holding her hand.

"Ita, Stiche," Delia respondet. "Et fortasse etiam nobis futura est historia amoris."

"Yes, Stichus," Delia responds. "And perhaps we, too, will have a love story in the future."

In villa nova Marci et Lydiae, omnia tranquilla et felicia sunt. Amor, qui olim in dubio erat, nunc fortis et stabilis est. Stichus et Delia, qui in hac historia magnam partem habuerunt, de futuris suis cogitant.

In Marcus and Lydia's new villa, everything is peaceful and happy. The love that was once in doubt is now strong and stable. Stichus and Delia, who played a big part in this story, think about their own futures.

"Fortasse et nos in futuro similem historiam amoris habebimus," Stichus ad Deliam dicit, in caelum stellatum spectans.

"Perhaps we too will have a similar love story in the future," Stichus says to Delia, looking at the starry sky.

Et sic, in fabula "Servus Astutus," finis est felix. Marcus et Lydia, in amore et felicitate, vitam novam incipiunt. Stichus et Delia, spectantes et subridendo, in futurum plenum amoris et gaudii sperant. Amor, ut semper, victor est.

And so, in the story "The Clever Servant," the ending is a happy one. Marcus and Lydia, in love and happiness, begin a new life. Stichus and Delia, watching and smiling, hope for a future full of love and joy. Love, as always, is the victor.

Servus Callidus

Capitulum I: In Via Romana

In urbe Roma, sub sole clarissimo, Balbus, mercator Romanus, per vias ambulat. Cum sacculo pleno nummorum, ad forum destinatus, negotium magni momenti gerere paratus est.

In the city of Rome, under the bright sun, Balbus, a Roman merchant, walks through the streets. With a bag full of coins, heading for the forum, he is ready to conduct an important business deal.

Balbus, gravis et serius, per viam festinat, sacculum bene clausum tenens. "Hodie in foro multum negotii faciam," secum cogitat, gressus suos accelerans.

Balbus, serious and focused, hurries down the road, holding his bag tightly closed. "Today, I will do a lot of business in the forum," he thinks to himself, quickening his pace.

Sosia, servus Balbi, callidus et astutus, dominum sequitur. Oculi eius circumspiciunt, semper vigilans. "Domine, cura ut sacculum tuum bene custodias," Sosia monens dicit.

Sosia, Balbus's clever and sharp-witted servant, follows his master. His eyes scan the surroundings, always alert. "Master, make sure to keep your bag well guarded," Sosia warns.

"Curate, Sosia, ego custodiam," Balbus respondet, sacculi custodiam suscipiens. Balbus Sosiae fidem habet, sed tamen sollicitus est.

"Don't worry, Sosia, I'll guard it," Balbus replies, taking care of the bag. Balbus trusts Sosia, but he is still anxious.

Dum per vias urbis ambulant, viam errant et in vicum ignotum deveniunt. Vicus est plenus hominum et tabernarum, sed Balbus et Sosia locum non recognoscunt.

As they walk through the streets of the city, they lose their way and end up in an unfamiliar alley. The alley is full of people and shops, but Balbus and Sosia do not recognize the place.

Ibi, hominem mendacem, Gaium nomine, conveniunt. Gaius, qui se divitem esse mentitur, ad eos accedit. "Salvete, peregrini! Ego sum Gaius, dives huius vici," blande dicit.

There, they meet a deceitful man named Gaius. Gaius, who lies about being wealthy, approaches them. "Greetings, travelers! I am Gaius, the rich man of this district," he says smoothly.

Sosia, verba Gaii audiens, eum suspectat. "Domine, hic homo nobis non fidus videtur," submisse ad Balbum dicit. Sed Balbus, Gaium hospitalem putans, eum ad cenam invitat.

Sosia, hearing Gaius's words, becomes suspicious of him. "Master, this man doesn't seem trustworthy," he quietly says to Balbus. But Balbus, thinking Gaius is being hospitable, invites him to dinner.

"Gaius, nobiscum ad cenam venias. Hospitalitatem tuam grate accipimus," Balbus, nihil mali suspicans, inquit. Sosia, licet sollicitus, domino suo obtemperat.

"Gaius, come to dinner with us. We gladly accept your hospitality," Balbus says, suspecting nothing. Sosia, though worried, obeys his master.

Gaius, invitationem acceptans, "Libenter, domine! Vos in domum meam ducam," respondet. Sosia, callidus et cautus, omnia observat, paratus ad quodlibet mendacium Gaii detegendum.

Gaius, accepting the invitation, responds, "Gladly, sir! I will take you to my house." Sosia, clever and cautious, observes everything, ready to uncover any lies from Gaius.

Et sic incipit fabula "Servus Callidus," cum Balbus, Sosia, et Gaius, tres diversae naturae homines, in vico Romano se inveniunt. Quid futurum sit in hac cena, nemo scit, sed Sosia, servus callidus, ad omnia paratus est.

And so begins the story "The Clever Servant," with Balbus, Sosia, and Gaius, three men of different characters, finding themselves in a Roman alley. What will happen at this dinner, no one knows, but Sosia, the clever servant, is prepared for anything.

# Capitulum II: Consilium Callidi Servi

In fabula "Servus Callidus," Sosia, servus Balbi, consilium capit ut dominus ne fallatur. Gaius mendax est, sed Balbus eum admirat et ei credit.

In the story "The Clever Servant," Sosia, the servant of Balbus, devises a plan to prevent his master from being deceived. Gaius is a liar, but Balbus admires and trusts him.

Sosia, dominum suum ad Gaii domum sequens, sollicitus est. "Domine, timeo ne Gaius nos decipiat. Non est qui se praestat esse," Sosia caute ad Balbum dicit.

Sosia, following his master to Gaius's house, is worried. "Master, I fear that Gaius will deceive us. He is not who he pretends to be," Sosia cautiously says to Balbus.

Balbus tamen Sosiae verba non credit et Gaium laudat. "Sosia, Gaius nobis amicus videtur. Cur eum suspectas?" Balbus interrogat.

However, Balbus does not believe Sosia's words and praises Gaius. "Sosia, Gaius seems to be a friend to us. Why are you suspicious of him?" Balbus asks.

Sosia, videns dominum suum non persuaderi, cum amico suo, Dromo nomine, consilium format. Dromo est servus alterius domini in vico et Sosiae amicus.

Sosia, seeing that his master is not convinced, forms a plan with his friend, named Dromo. Dromo is a servant of another master in the neighborhood and a friend of Sosia.

"Dromo, adiuva me Gaium mendacem detegere. Dominus meus ei credit, sed ego non," Sosia rogat, cum Dromo in angulo viae colloquens.

"Dromo, help me expose Gaius the liar. My master trusts him, but I do not," Sosia asks, speaking with Dromo in a corner of the street.

Dromo, callidus et vivax, consensum dat. "Sosia, tecum ero. Inveniemus veritatem," Dromo respondet, paratus ad iuvandum.

Dromo, clever and lively, agrees. "Sosia, I will be with you. We will find the truth," Dromo responds, ready to help.

Nocte, cum luna clara et stellae micantes, Sosia et Dromo furtim ad Gaii domum pergunt. Domus obscura et silens est, non divitis domus similis.

At night, with the bright moon and twinkling stars, Sosia and Dromo sneak to Gaius's house. The house is dark and silent, not like the house of a rich man.

Intrant domum Gaii et mox inveniunt eum pauperem esse. Domus est vacua et vix ulla ornamenta habet. "Vide, Dromo, Gaius pauper est! Omnia mendacia sunt!" Sosia susurrat.

They enter Gaius's house and soon find that he is poor. The house is empty and has hardly any decorations. "Look, Dromo, Gaius is poor! It's all lies!" Sosia whispers.

Sosia et Dromo, re vera cognita, consilium habent ut Balbum de Gaii mendaciis moneant. "Domino nostro veritatem dicemus," Sosia statuit, plenus certitudine.

Sosia and Dromo, having learned the truth, make a plan to warn Balbus about Gaius's lies. "We will tell our master the truth," Sosia decides, full of certainty.

Dromo, "Ego te adiuvabo. Dominus tuus scire debet," inquit, Sosiae in consilio adhaerens.

Dromo says, "I will help you. Your master must know," supporting Sosia in the plan.

Cum aurora appropinquat, Sosia et Dromo parati sunt ad veritatem Balbo revelandam. "Domine, parati sumus tibi omnia demonstrare," Sosia dicit, cum primum Balbum conveniunt.

As dawn approaches, Sosia and Dromo are ready to reveal the truth to Balbus. "Master, we are ready to show you everything," Sosia says when they first meet Balbus.

Et sic, in capitulo secundo "Servus Callidus," Sosia et Dromo, duo servi callidi, se parant ad dominum suum a deceptione liberandum. Quomodo Balbus ad hanc revelationem respondebit, et quid de Gaii mendaciis fiet, in sequentibus capitulis apparebit.

And so, in the second chapter of "The Clever Servant," Sosia and Dromo, two clever servants, prepare to free their master from deception. How Balbus will respond to this revelation, and what will happen to Gaius's lies, will be revealed in the following chapters.

Capitulum III: Cena et Mendacia

In domo Balbi, opulentus mercator Romanus, magna cena paratur. Gaius, mendax de quo Sosia et Dromo veritatem invenire cupiunt, ad cenam invitatus est.

In the house of Balbus, a wealthy Roman merchant, a grand dinner is being prepared. Gaius, the liar about whom Sosia and Dromo wish to discover the truth, has been invited to the dinner.

In magnifico triclinio, ubi cena fit, Gaius fabulas de divitiis suis narrat. "In villis meis, servi centum laborant," inquit, vinum in calice suo spectans.

In the magnificent dining room where the dinner takes place, Gaius tells stories about his wealth. "In my estates, a hundred servants work," he says, gazing at the wine in his cup.

Balbus, hospes generosus et credulus, Gaii fabulis credit et magna cum laetitia audit. "O Gaie, fortunatus es! Tales divitias habere," Balbus admirans dicit.

Balbus, a generous and gullible host, believes Gaius's stories and listens with great delight. "Oh Gaius, you are fortunate! To have such wealth," Balbus says admiringly.

Sosia et Dromo, servi callidi, in angulo triclinii consilium capiunt. Sosia, oculis in Gaium fixis, "Mox Gaius mendax revelabitur," susurrat.

Sosia and Dromo, the clever servants, form a plan in the corner of the dining room. Sosia, his eyes fixed on Gaius, whispers, "Soon the liar Gaius will be revealed."

Dromo, paratus ad signum dandum, "Ego signum dabo. Parati estote," respondet, oculis ludentibus.

Dromo, ready to give the signal, responds, "I will give the signal. Be ready," his eyes gleaming.

Cena procedit et Gaius plura mendacia narrat. "In agris meis, vinum optimum producitur," inquit, risu suo falsum celans.

The dinner proceeds, and Gaius tells more lies. "In my fields, the finest wine is produced," he says, hiding his falsehood with a smile.

Dromo, tempus esse sentiens, signum subtile dat. Subito, lumen in triclinio extinguitur et omnes in tenebris sedent.

Dromo, sensing it is time, gives a subtle signal. Suddenly, the lights in the dining room go out, and everyone sits in darkness.

In tenebris, Sosia rapide ad Gaium movet et eius sacculum, in quo nummi esse putantur, furat. "Nunc veritas apparebit," Sosia subridens dicit.

In the darkness, Sosia quickly moves to Gaius and steals his bag, where coins are thought to be. "Now the truth will appear," Sosia says with a grin.

Cum lumen rursus accenditur, Sosia in medio triclinii stat, sacculum Gaii tenens. "Ecce, Gaius pauper est!" clamat, sacculum aperiens. Omnes ad Sosiam spectant, stupore affecti.

When the light is turned on again, Sosia stands in the middle of the dining room, holding Gaius's bag. "Behold, Gaius is poor!" he shouts, opening the bag. Everyone looks at Sosia, stunned.

Sacculum vacuum est, nulli nummi in eo sunt. Gaius, rubore in vultu, nihil respondet. Balbus, re vera cognita, iratus et confusus est.

The bag is empty; there are no coins inside. Gaius, his face red with embarrassment, says nothing. Balbus, now knowing the truth, is angry and confused.

"O Gaie, mendax fuisti! Nos omnes fefellisti," Balbus exclamat, Gaium accusans.

"Oh Gaius, you were a liar! You deceived us all," Balbus exclaims, accusing Gaius.

Et sic, in capitulo tertio "Servus Callidus," Sosia et Dromo, consilio astuto usi, veritatem de Gaii mendaciis revelant. Balbus, deceptus sed nunc edoctus, Gaium ex domo sua expellit. Sosia et Dromo, sui consilii successu laetantes, ad invicem subridendo sciunt se dominum suum a fallacia servavisse.

And so, in the third chapter of "The Clever Servant," Sosia and Dromo, using a clever plan, reveal the truth about Gaius's lies. Balbus, deceived but now enlightened, expels Gaius from his house. Sosia and Dromo, rejoicing in the success of their plan, smile at each other, knowing they have saved their master from deceit.

Capitulum IV: Gaius Confunditur

In domo Balbi, res tumultuosa evenit. Cena, quae coepta est cum laetitia et convivio, nunc vertitur in confusionem et revelationem.

In the house of Balbus, a tumultuous event occurs. The dinner, which began with joy and celebration, now turns into confusion and revelation.

Balbus, nunc videns Gaium mendacem esse, ira commotus est. "Gai, quid hoc est? Ubi sunt divitiae de quibus locutus es?" interrogat, voce severa.

Balbus, now seeing that Gaius is a liar, is stirred with anger. "Gaius, what is this? Where is the wealth you spoke of?" he asks in a stern voice.

Gaius, nunc in angulo pressus, confunditur. Verba eius deficiunt, et vultus eius veritatem prodit. "Ego... ego..." incipit, sed nihil complet.

Gaius, now cornered, is confused. His words fail him, and his face reveals the truth. "I... I..." he begins, but finishes nothing.

Sosia, ad Balbum accedens, "Domine, te monui de Gaii mendaciis. Nunc veritas patet," dicit, tranquille stans.

Sosia, approaching Balbus, says, "Master, I warned you about Gaius's lies. Now the truth is clear," standing calmly.

Balbus, ira adhuc in vultu, Gaium a cena expellit. "Gai, exi domo mea! Mendaces hic non toleramus," exclamat.

Balbus, still with anger on his face, expels Gaius from the dinner. "Gaius, leave my house! We do not tolerate liars here," he exclaims.

Sosia et Dromo, consilii sui successu, inter se rident. "Vidisti, Dromo? Veritas in luce est," Sosia subridens dicit.

Sosia and Dromo, pleased with the success of their plan, laugh together. "Did you see, Dromo? The truth is in the light," Sosia says, smiling.

Balbus, ad Sosiam conversus, "Sosia, tibi gratias ago. Servus callidus es et fidelis," laudat, gratitudinem suam ostendens.

Balbus, turning to Sosia, says, "Sosia, I thank you. You are a clever and loyal servant," showing his gratitude.

Gaius, confusus et humilatus, a cena discedit. Caput suum demissum habet, et tacitus est. Omnes spectant eum exire, silentium in triclinio regnat.

Gaius, confused and humiliated, leaves the dinner. He has his head down and is silent. Everyone watches him leave, and silence reigns in the dining room.

Balbus, ad omnes convivas, "Hac in domo, semper veritatem loquimini. Mendacia non feremus," conclamat, principium suum affirmans.

Balbus, to all the guests, declares, "In this house, always speak the truth. We will not tolerate lies," affirming his principle.

Et sic finit caput quartum "Servus Callidus." Balbus, nunc edoctus de mendaciis Gaii, gratiam habet pro Sosia et Dromo, qui veritatem revelaverunt. Sosia et Dromo, suae astutiae victores, ad invicem subridendo, laetantur quod dominum suum a deceptione servaverunt. Gaius, mendax confusus, discedit, et lectionem de veritate accepit.

And so ends the fourth chapter of "The Clever Servant." Balbus, now enlightened about Gaius's lies, is grateful to Sosia and Dromo, who revealed the truth. Sosia and Dromo, victorious in their cleverness, smile at each other, happy that they saved their master from deception. Gaius, the confused liar, leaves, having learned a lesson about truth.

Capitulum V: Nova Negotia

Post incidentem cum Gaio, mercatore mendace, Balbus, mercator Romanus, novis rebus intendit. Ad forum Romanum it, ubi novam mercaturam molitur.

After the incident with Gaius, the deceitful merchant, Balbus, a Roman merchant, focuses on new matters. He goes to the Roman forum, where he plans new business.

Cum mane clarescit, Balbus et Sosia, servus eius, iter ad forum incipiunt. "Hodie novum initium faciemus," Balbus, sacculum nummorum portans, dicit.

As morning dawns, Balbus and Sosia, his servant, begin their journey to the forum. "Today we will make a fresh start," Balbus says, carrying a bag of coins.

Sosia, secum ambulans, monitionem offert. "Domine, post Gaii fraudem, cautiores simus. Non omnes in foro fidi sunt," Sosia prudente voce dicit.

Sosia, walking beside him, offers a warning. "Master, after Gaius's fraud, let us be more cautious. Not everyone in the forum is trustworthy," Sosia says wisely.

Balbus, ad forum appropinquans, "Sosia, recte dicis. Sed bonam mercaturam facere cupio. Negotium nostrum augere debemus," inquit.

Balbus, approaching the forum, says, "Sosia, you are right. But I want to make a good deal. We must expand our business."

Sosia, caput inclinans, novum negotium proponit. "Quid si vinum bonum emamus et vendamus? Vinum semper in pretio est," suadet.

Sosia, bowing his head, proposes a new venture. "What if we buy good wine and sell it? Wine is always in demand," he suggests.

Balbus, Sosiae consilium audiens, "Hmm, idea bona est, Sosia. Vinum bonum semper quaeritur. Consilium tuum probamus," respondet.

Balbus, hearing Sosia's advice, responds, "Hmm, that's a good idea, Sosia. Good wine is always sought after. I approve of your plan."

In foro, ubi homines et mercatores convenerunt, Balbus et Sosia inter tabernas et mercatores ambulant. Multa sunt bona venalia, sed in vinum bonum intendunt.

In the forum, where people and merchants have gathered, Balbus and Sosia walk between the stalls and sellers. There are many goods for sale, but they focus on finding good wine.

Post multas disceptationes et colloquia, bonum vinum ad bonum pretium emunt. "Videtis, Sosia, hoc vinum excellens est. Bene vendetur," Balbus, inspecto vino, dicit.

After many negotiations and conversations, they buy good wine at a good price. "See, Sosia, this wine is excellent. It will sell well," Balbus says, inspecting the wine.

Sosia, vina in sacculis spectans, "Hoc negotium prosperum erit, domine. Vinum semper desideratur," confirmat.

Sosia, looking at the wine in the bags, confirms, "This business will be successful, master. Wine is always in demand."

Cum sol meridiem tangit et forum adhuc plenum est hominum, Balbus, ad Sosiam conversus, "Gratias tibi, Sosia, pro sapientia tua. Sine te, haec mercatura non fieret," gratias agit.

As the sun reaches noon and the forum is still full of people, Balbus, turning to Sosia, says, "Thank you, Sosia, for your wisdom. Without you, this deal would not have happened," expressing his gratitude.

Et sic, in Capitulo V "Servus Callidus," Balbus et Sosia, novum negotium incipiunt. Sosia, servus callidus et fidelis, ducem in mercatura bonam prae se fert, et Balbus, dominus eius, in sapientia servi sui confidit. Nova via ad prosperitatem et successum aperta est.

And so, in Chapter V of "The Clever Servant," Balbus and Sosia begin a new venture. Sosia, the clever and loyal servant, leads the way to a good deal, and Balbus, his master, trusts in his servant's wisdom. A new path to prosperity and success has been opened.

Capitulum VI: Negotium Crescit

In fabula "Servus Callidus," negotium vini, quod Balbus et Sosia coeperunt, mirabiliter crescit. Vinum quod emerunt in foro bene venditur, et paulatim divites fiunt.

In the story "The Clever Servant," the wine business that Balbus and Sosia started grows remarkably. The wine they bought in the forum sells well, and gradually they become wealthy.

Balbus et Sosia nunc in villa nova, pulchra et ampla, habitant. Domus eorum est signum prosperitatis et successus in negotiis.

Balbus and Sosia now live in a new, beautiful, and spacious villa. Their home is a symbol of prosperity and success in business.

Sosia, plus quam servus, nunc administrator prudentissimus fit. Omnia negotia curat, dum Balbus ad forum it ad mercaturas novas faciendas.

Sosia, more than just a servant, now becomes a very wise manager. He takes care of all the business, while Balbus goes to the forum to make new trades.

Uno die, cum sol in caelo altus est, Balbus ad Sosiam, qui in atrio sedet, accedit: "Sosia, sine te, haec omnia non fierent. Tibi maximas gratias ago," dicit.

One day, when the sun is high in the sky, Balbus approaches Sosia, who is sitting in the atrium: "Sosia, without you, none of this would have happened. I thank you very much," he says.

Subito, Dromo, amicus Sosiae et servus in vicinia, ad villam currens venit. "Sosia! Balbe! Audite! Vicus noster celeber fit propter vinum nostrum!" Dromo, anhelans, exclamat.

Suddenly, Dromo, Sosia's friend and a servant in the neighborhood, comes running to the villa. "Sosia! Balbus! Listen! Our village is becoming famous because of our wine!" Dromo exclaims, panting.

"Dromo, quid dicis? Vicus noster?" Sosia miratus interrogat.

"Dromo, what are you saying? Our village?" Sosia asks, surprised.

"Etiam! Omnes de vino nostro loquuntur. Festum magnum in vico fit!" Dromo respondet, vultu laeto.

"Yes! Everyone is talking about our wine. A great festival is happening in the village!" Dromo replies, his face joyful.

In vico, ubi festum fit, omnes convivae laeti sunt. Musica sonat, et homines cantant et saltant. Vinum Balbi et Sosiae in medio est, causa laetitiae.

In the village, where the festival takes place, all the guests are joyful. Music plays, and people sing and dance. Balbus and Sosia's wine is at the center, the cause of the joy.

Sosia et Balbus, in festo honorati, inter convivas ambulant. "Videtis, Sosia, quid una facere potuimus!" Balbus dicit, circumspiciens.

Sosia and Balbus, honored at the festival, walk among the guests. "You see, Sosia, what we could achieve together!" Balbus says, looking around.

"Vere, domine. Nos fecimus hanc rem magnam," Sosia respondet, cum gaudio.

"Truly, master. We made this great thing happen," Sosia responds, with joy.

Cum festum ad summum venit, Balbus ad populum: "Gratias vobis omnes! Sine vobis, hoc non fieret. Vinum nostrum, vinum vici nostri!" clamat, calicem suum tollens.

As the festival reaches its peak, Balbus addresses the people: "Thank you all! Without you, this wouldn't have happened. Our wine, the wine of our village!" he shouts, raising his cup.

Et sic, in Capitulo VI "Servus Callidus," Balbus et Sosia, per industriam et sapientiam, non solum divites fiunt sed etiam in vico suo honorantur. Eorum negotium non solum prosperum est, sed etiam causa gaudii et unitatis in communitate. Sosia, servus olim humilis, nunc vir honoratus et laudatus est.

And so, in Chapter VI of "The Clever Servant," Balbus and Sosia, through hard work and wisdom, not only become wealthy but are also honored in their village. Their business is not only successful but also a source of joy and unity in the community. Sosia, once a humble servant, is now a man honored and praised.

Capitulum VII: Invidia Vicini

In fabula "Servus Callidus," nova turbatio oritur. Lucius, vicinus Balbi et Sosiae, invidia motus est ob eorum successum in negotio vini.

In the story "The Clever Servant," a new disturbance arises. Lucius, the neighbor of Balbus and Sosia, is driven by envy because of their success in the wine business.

Lucius, homo ambitiosus sed minus prudens, per viam ambulat, cogitans de divitiis novis Balbi et Sosiae. "Quomodo Balbus et Sosia tam divites fiunt?" Lucius se interrogat, frontem contractus.

Lucius, an ambitious but less wise man, walks down the street, thinking about the newfound wealth of Balbus and Sosia. "How did Balbus and Sosia become so rich?" Lucius asks himself, furrowing his brow.

Frustratus et zelotypus, Lucius consilium capit. "Ego vinum melius emam et illos superabo. Ostendam me esse mercatorem potentiorum!" Lucius statuit, animo pleno ambitionis.

Frustrated and jealous, Lucius forms a plan. "I will buy better wine and surpass them. I will show that I am a more powerful merchant!" Lucius decides, with a mind full of ambition.

Sosia, qui semper vigilans et callidus est, Lucii consilium audit. "Domine, Lucius nos superare vult. Audivi eum in foro loquentem," Sosia, ad Balbum in villa nova eorum conversus, dicit.

Sosia, who is always watchful and clever, overhears Lucius's plan. "Master, Lucius wants to surpass us. I heard him talking in the forum," Sosia says, turning to Balbus in their new villa.

Balbus, audito hoc, "Cauti simus, Sosia, sed non timeamus. Negotium nostrum in honore et honestate fundatum est," respondet.

Balbus, upon hearing this, replies, "Let's be cautious, Sosia, but not afraid. Our business is founded on honor and honesty."

Lucius, in sua avaritia et invidia, ad forum it et vinum malum emere conatur, putans se posse Balbum et Sosiam superare. Sed non novit de vino sicut illi.

Lucius, driven by his greed and envy, goes to the forum and tries to buy bad wine, thinking he can surpass Balbus and Sosia. But he doesn't know as much about wine as they do.

Sosia et Balbus, Lucii consilia cognoscentes, inter se in villa sua ridere. "Lucius non intellegit quid in vino bono sit," Sosia subridens dicit.

Sosia and Balbus, knowing Lucius's plans, laugh together in their villa. "Lucius doesn't understand what makes good wine," Sosia says with a smile.

"Verum," Balbus assentitur. "Nos in nostro consilio et labore permanebimus. Semper astuti et honesti simus."

"True," Balbus agrees. "We will stay with our plan and hard work. Let us always be clever and honest."

Lucius, vinum emens, se putat futurum esse potentiorum Balbo et Sosiae. Sed non habet scientiam nec sapientiam quam illi habent.

Lucius, buying the wine, thinks he will become more powerful than Balbus and Sosia. But he doesn't have the knowledge or wisdom that they have.

Et sic finit Capitulum VII "Servus Callidus." Balbus et Sosia, sua prudentia et diligentia usi, in negocio suo manent, non perturbati a conatibus invidi vicini. Lucius, suo consilio deficienti, in sua invidia et ambitione manet, sed non potest superare ingenium et honestatem Balbi et Sosiae.

And so ends Chapter VII of "The Clever Servant." Balbus and Sosia, using their prudence and diligence, remain steady in their business, undisturbed by the efforts of their envious neighbor. Lucius, with his failing plan, remains in his envy and ambition but cannot surpass the intelligence and honesty of Balbus and Sosia.

Capitulum VIII: Fallacia Lucii

In vico Romano, Lucius, vicinus Balbi et Sosiae, vinum malum vendere conatur. Tabernam suam apertam habet et vinum in amphoris posuit. Sed nemo ad tabernam Lucii accedit. Homines vinum eius spectant, sed mox abeunt. Ita Lucius solus cum vino suo manet.

In the Roman village, Lucius, the neighbor of Balbus and Sosia, tries to sell bad wine. He has his shop open and has placed the wine in amphoras. But no one comes to Lucius's shop. People look at his wine, but soon leave. Thus Lucius remains alone with his wine.

Cum sol in caelo altus est, Lucius frustratur quod nemo vinum emere vult. Iratus, per vias ambulat et de Balbo cogitat. "Cur omnes vinum Balbi emunt? Vinum meum nemo emere vult!" clamat Lucius.

When the sun is high in the sky, Lucius becomes frustrated because no one wants to buy his wine. Angry, he walks through the streets and thinks about Balbus. "Why is everyone buying Balbus's wine? No one wants to buy my wine!" Lucius shouts.

Sosia, qui prope stat, Lucium audire potest et ad Lucium accedit ut eum consoletur. "Luci, honestas melior est quam fallacia. Vinum tuum malum est, populus scit," Sosia placide dicit.

Sosia, who stands nearby, can hear Lucius and approaches to comfort him. "Lucius, honesty is better than deceit. Your wine is bad, and the people know it," Sosia says calmly.

Lucius caput demittit et consilii mali paenitet. "Ego stultus fui. Vinum malum vendere volui. Nunc nihil habeo," tristis Lucius dicit.

Lucius lowers his head and regrets his bad plan. "I was foolish. I wanted to sell bad wine. Now I have nothing," Lucius says sadly.

Balbus, qui advenit, Sosiam et Lucium audit et Lucio auxilium offert. "Luci, te adiuvare possumus. Veni, tecum laborare possumus," Balbus amice dicit.

Balbus, who arrives, hears Sosia and Lucius and offers help to Lucius. "Lucius, we can help you. Come, we can work together," Balbus says kindly.

Lucius, oculos levans, Balbum et Sosiam spectat et respondet, "Gratias vobis, me errasse agnosco. Auxilium vestrum accipio," Lucius, paenitentia motus, dicit.

Lucius, raising his eyes, looks at Balbus and Sosia and replies, "Thank you both, I acknowledge my mistake. I accept your help," Lucius says, moved by repentance.

Lucius, Balbo et Sosiae amicus fit. Una laborant et vinum bonum faciunt. Balbus, ad omnes spectans, dicit, "Una fortiores sumus. Honestas et labor nobis bonum vinum dant." Lucius et Sosia cum Balbo ridere incipiunt. In vico, unitas et amicitia regnant.

Lucius becomes a friend to Balbus and Sosia. They work together and make good wine. Balbus, looking at everyone, says, "Together we are stronger. Honesty and hard work give us good wine." Lucius and Sosia begin to laugh with Balbus. In the village, unity and friendship reign.

Et sic finit Capitulum VIII "Servus Callidus." Lucius, ex errore suo discit et amicus fit. Balbus et Sosia, sua bonitate, Lucium adiuvant. In vico, omnes nunc sciant honestatem et fructus laboris esse meliores quam fallaciam et invidiam.

And so ends Chapter VIII of "The Clever Servant." Lucius learns from his mistake and becomes a friend. Balbus and Sosia, in their kindness, help Lucius. In the village, everyone now knows that honesty and the fruits of hard work are better than deceit and envy.

Capitulum IX: Prosperitas et Amicitia

Balbus, Sosia, et Lucius nunc una laborant. Post fallaciam Lucii, nova societas inter eos nata est. Haec societas prospera est et omnes in vico eam laudant.

Balbus, Sosia, and Lucius now work together. After Lucius's deceit, a new partnership was formed between them. This partnership is prosperous, and everyone in the village praises it.

In foro Romano, vinum quod Balbus, Sosia, et Lucius faciunt, maxime laudatur. Multi ad tabernam eorum veniunt et vinum emunt. "Videtis," inquit Balbus, vinum vendens, "amicitia et labor bonum fructum ferunt."

In the Roman forum, the wine that Balbus, Sosia, and Lucius make is highly praised. Many come to their shop and buy wine. "You see," says Balbus, selling the wine, "friendship and hard work bring good results."

Sosia, vinum in amphoras ponens, addit: "Et honestas semper vincit." Lucius, qui nuper societati adiunctus est, adstantibus dicit: "Amicos bonos habere vera felicitas est."

Sosia, putting wine into the amphoras, adds: "And honesty always wins." Lucius, who recently joined the partnership, says to the bystanders: "Having good friends is true happiness."

Balbus et Sosia, gaudio pleni, festum magnificum in villa nova parant. Omnes vicinos et amicos invitant. "Hodie festum facimus!" exclamat Balbus.

Balbus and Sosia, full of joy, prepare a grand feast in their new villa. They invite all the neighbors and friends. "Today we celebrate!" exclaims Balbus.

Die festi, villa nova splendet. Omnes vicini et amici ad festum conveniunt. Musica sonat; homines cantant et saltant. Vinum eorum in omnium calicibus est.

On the day of the feast, the new villa shines. All the neighbors and friends gather for the celebration. Music plays; people sing and dance. Their wine fills everyone's cups.

Sosia, inter convivas ambulans, dicit: "Vita est brevis, amicitiam colamus." Omnes ad Sosiam spectant et assentiunt.

Sosia, walking among the guests, says: "Life is short, let us cultivate friendship." Everyone looks at Sosia and agrees.

Balbus, cum calice vini in manu, ad omnes conclamat: "Et semper bene agamus!" Convivae plaudunt; omnes laeti sunt.

Balbus, with a cup of wine in hand, calls out to everyone: "And let us always do good!" The guests applaud; everyone is happy.

Et sic finit Capitulum IX "Servus Callidus." Per amicitiam et societatem, Balbus, Sosia, et Lucius prosperant. In foro et in vico, vinum eorum et amicitia celebrantur. Omnes discunt honestatem, laborem, et amicitiam esse viam ad veram felicitatem et prosperitatem.

And so ends Chapter IX of "The Clever Servant." Through friendship and partnership, Balbus, Sosia, and Lucius thrive. In the forum and the village, their wine and friendship are celebrated. Everyone learns that honesty, hard work, and friendship are the path to true happiness and prosperity.

Capitulum X: Felicitas Continua

Balbus, Sosia, et Lucius diu felices vivunt. Negotium vinarii eorum per multas terras extenditur et floret. Villa eorum fit locus amicitiae et laetitiae, ubi convivae saepe conveniunt.

Balbus, Sosia, and Lucius live happily for a long time. Their wine business extends across many lands and thrives. Their villa becomes a place of friendship and joy, where guests often gather.

Quodam die, in horto villae, Sosia amphoram vini portans inquit, "Bene est cum domino bono servire." Lucius, qui prope stat, ridet et ad Sosiam dicit, "Et cum servo fideli laborare verum est."

One day, in the villa's garden, Sosia, carrying a jar of wine, says, "It is good to serve a good master." Lucius, standing nearby, laughs and says to Sosia, "And to work with a loyal servant is true."

Balbus, qui ad eos accedit, "Et cum amicis veris vivere," addit. Circumspiciunt et de fortuna felicitateque sua cogitant.

Balbus, who approaches them, adds, "And to live with true friends." They look around and reflect on their fortune and happiness.

Infantes Balbi, Sosiae, et Lucii in horto una ludunt, rident et clamant, eorumque risus per hortum resonat. "Generatio futura spem nobis dat," Balbus, infantes spectans, dicit.

The children of Balbus, Sosia, and Lucius play together in the garden, laughing and shouting, and their laughter echoes through the garden. "The future generation gives us hope," Balbus says, watching the children.

Subito, nubes obscurae in caelo apparent. Ventus incipit flare, et omnes in villa se ad tempestatem parant. Sed tempestas non venit, et sol iterum lucet.

Suddenly, dark clouds appear in the sky. The wind begins to blow, and everyone in the villa prepares for a storm. But the storm does not come, and the sun shines again.

"Videtis, etiam post nubila sol lucet," Sosia dicit. Balbus, ad caelum spectans, "Sic in vita, post difficultates, semper spes est," inquit.

"You see, even after clouds, the sun shines," Sosia says. Balbus, looking at the sky, says, "So it is in life, after difficulties, there is always hope."

Omnes in villa convocantur et de futuris consiliis colloquuntur. Decidunt ut plures terras viserent et novas societates in aliis locis facerent.

Everyone in the villa gathers, and they discuss future plans. They decide to visit more lands and establish new partnerships in other places.

Die quodam, magna navis ad portum villae appropinquat. Balbus, Sosia, et Lucius in portu stant, de nova pericula excitati. "Nunc ad novas terras navigabimus," Balbus exclamat.

One day, a large ship approaches the villa's port. Balbus, Sosia, and Lucius stand in the port, excited about new adventures. "Now we will sail to new lands," Balbus exclaims.

Eorum filii et filiae, qui iam adulti sunt, in villa remanent et negotium curant. "Nostri liberi iam nos adiuvare possunt," Sosia dicit.

Their sons and daughters, who are now adults, remain in the villa and take care of the business. "Our children can help us now," Sosia says.

Ante discessum, magna cena in villa fit. "Hodie novum caput in vita nostra celebramus," Lucius dicit. "Et semper memores erimus unde venimus," Balbus addit.

Before their departure, a great feast is held in the villa. "Today we celebrate a new chapter in our lives," Lucius says. "And we will always remember where we came from," Balbus adds.

Cum luna in caelo alta est, Balbus, Sosia, et Lucius ad navem ambulant. Omnes in villa eos ad portum comitantur et "Vale!" dicunt.

With the moon high in the sky, Balbus, Sosia, and Lucius walk to the ship. Everyone in the villa accompanies them to the port and says, "Farewell!"

Navigant per mare magnum, terras novas explorant, amicitias novas faciunt, et semper de vico suo et familia memores sunt. Eorum vita, plena periculis et felicitate, exemplum est quomodo honestas, labor, et amicitia viam ad veram felicitatem et prosperitatem monstrant.

They sail across the great sea, explore new lands, make new friendships, and always remember their village and family. Their life, full of dangers and happiness, is an example of how honesty, hard work, and friendship show the way to true happiness and prosperity.

Et sic finitur fabula "Servus Callidus." Balbus, Sosia, et Lucius, per multos annos felices vivunt, et eorum vita laetitia amicitiaque plena est. Narratio eorum ostendit quomodo amicitia, labor, et honestas in vita maximi sint.

And so the story "The Clever Servant" ends. Balbus, Sosia, and Lucius live happily for many years, and their lives are full of joy and friendship. Their story shows how friendship, hard work, and honesty are of the greatest importance in life.

Claudius in Britannia militat

Capitulum Primum: In Litus Manicae

Claudius, legionarius fortis et audax, ad litus Manicae se parabat. Sol altus in caelo erat, ventusque leniter flabat. Cum aliis militibus, castra militaria robusta constituebat.

Claudius, a brave and bold legionary, was preparing himself at the shore of the English Channel. The sun was high in the sky, and a gentle breeze was blowing. With the other soldiers, he was setting up strong military camps.

"Videte, fratres," Claudius exclamavit, "Hae naves longae nos ad Britanniam ferent! Gloria et honores nobis manent!"

"Look, brothers," Claudius exclaimed, "These long ships will carry us to Britain! Glory and honors await us!"

Miles proximus, nomine Gaius, ad Claudium accessit et dixit, "Ita vero, sed proelia dura nobis sunt. Num times, Claudius?"

A nearby soldier, named Gaius, approached Claudius and said, "Indeed, but hard battles lie ahead of us. Are you afraid, Claudius?"

Claudius risit et respondit, "Timor? Non est in corde Romanorum! Caesar nos ducet et victoria nostra erit."

Claudius laughed and replied, "Fear? It is not in the heart of Romans! Caesar will lead us, and victory will be ours."

Subito, nubes obscurae caelum texerunt, et tempestas magna appropinquabat. Claudius et milites celeriter arma et cibum collegerunt, parati ad quodcumque veniret.

Suddenly, dark clouds covered the sky, and a great storm was approaching. Claudius and the soldiers quickly gathered their weapons and food, prepared for whatever might come.

"Nocte hac," Claudius in tabernaculo suo meditabatur, "de patria et familia mea cogito. Quam dulcis est Roma, quam cari sunt mihi mei!"

"Tonight," Claudius reflected in his tent, "I think of my homeland and my family. How sweet is Rome, how dear are my loved ones!"

Extra, Galli auxiliares, qui cum Romanis erant, de terra natali sua narrabant. Eorum verba de silvis vastis et fluminibus magnis erant.

Outside, the Gallic auxiliaries, who were with the Romans, were talking about their homeland. Their words were about vast forests and great rivers.

Claudius heard them and said, "Oh Gauls, we praise your strength and friendship. We stand together!"

Tum, nuntius advenit et dixit, "Audite! Profectio nostra differtur. Tempestas navigare non sinit."

Then, a messenger arrived and said, "Listen! Our departure is delayed. The storm does not allow us to sail."

Militum murmur ortum est, sed disciplina Romana praevaluit. Omnes patienter exspectabant.

A murmur arose among the soldiers, but Roman discipline prevailed. Everyone waited patiently.

Die sequenti, cum sol rursus luceret, magnus Caesar ipse ad castra venit. Statura alta, vultu sereno, ad milites accessit.

The next day, when the sun shone again, the great Caesar himself came to the camp. Tall in stature, with a calm face, he approached the soldiers.

"O milites," Caesar coepit, "tempus adventum est. Britanniam invadere debemus. Fortes estote, et gloria aeterna erit vestra!"

"Oh soldiers," Caesar began, "the time has come. We must invade Britain. Be strong, and eternal glory will be yours!"

Militibus hortatis, Caesar signum dedit. Naves paratae erant, et milites, animo renovato, parati ad novas terras et nova proelia.

After encouraging the soldiers, Caesar gave the signal. The ships were ready, and the soldiers, with renewed spirit, were prepared for new lands and new battles.

Claudius, galeam suam induens, ad caelum aspexit et dixit, "Pro te, Roma, pro gloria, pro Caesare pugnabo!"

Claudius, putting on his helmet, looked up at the sky and said, "For you, Rome, for glory, for Caesar, I will fight!"

Et sic, capitulo primo finito, Claudius et sui commilitones ad novas periculas se parabant, corde forti et spe magna.

And so, with the first chapter concluded, Claudius and his comrades prepared for new dangers, with strong hearts and great hope.

Capitulum Secundum: Transitus Manici

Claudius, cum galea sua nitente et gladio acuto, in nave Caesaris navigabat. Mare undique eum circumdabat, nautaeque fortiter laborabant, quia mare valde turbidum erat.

Claudius, with his shining helmet and sharp sword, was sailing on Caesar's ship. The sea surrounded him on all sides, and the sailors worked hard because the sea was very rough.

"Certe, hoc mare non est amicum," Claudius Marcum, amicum suum, alloquebatur. "Sed Romani sumus! Neque mare neque hostes nos terrebunt!"

"Surely, this sea is not friendly," Claudius said to his friend Marcus. "But we are Romans! Neither the sea nor the enemies will frighten us!"

Procul in horizonte, subito, Britannia visa est. Terra viridis montesque alti, quos sol illuminabat, apparebant. Milites, cum Claudio in medio eorum, silentium servabant, animos ad futura proelia praeparantes.

Far off on the horizon, suddenly, Britain was seen. Green land and tall mountains, illuminated by the sun, appeared. The soldiers, with Claudius in their midst, maintained silence, preparing their minds for the battles to come.

Ecce! Repente, naves hostium apparuerunt, velis plenis vento. Omnes milites ad arma cucurrerunt, et Caesar ipse ordines dabat.

Look! Suddenly, enemy ships appeared, with sails full of wind. All the soldiers ran to their weapons, and Caesar himself was giving orders.

"Parati estote, milites!" Caesar exclamavit. "Hodie virtutem vestram ostendetis!"

"Be ready, soldiers!" Caesar exclaimed. "Today, you will show your courage!"

Conflictus cum hostibus coepit. Sagittae per aera volabant, et clamor magnus erat. Claudius, in prora stans, fortiter pugnabat. Gladius eius hostes terrebant, scutumque eius multos ictus sustinebat.

The battle with the enemies began. Arrows flew through the air, and there was a great clamor. Claudius, standing at the bow, fought bravely. His sword struck fear into the enemies, and his shield withstood many blows.

Subito, naves Britannicae, vi Romanorum victae, repulsae sunt. Sol rursus lucet, mareque paulatim tranquillatur.

Suddenly, the British ships, defeated by the might of the Romans, were pushed back. The sun shone again, and the sea gradually became calm.

"Victoria nostra est!" Claudius exclamavit, militesque laeti erant.

"Victory is ours!" Claudius exclaimed, and the soldiers were joyful.

Sed adhuc labor non finitus erat. Litus Britannicum appropinquabat, militesque ad descensum parabant. Tunc, a litore, saxa et sagittae a Britannis iactabantur.

But the work was not yet finished. The British shore was approaching, and the soldiers were preparing to disembark. Then, from the shore, rocks and arrows were thrown by the Britons.

"Ad pugnam, fratres!" Claudius clamavit. "Hodie aut victoriam aut gloriosam mortem!"

"To battle, brothers!" Claudius shouted. "Today, either victory or glorious death!"

Claudius primus ex nave in aquam saltavit, ceterique milites eum secuti sunt. Undae altae et frigidae erant, sed milites, virtute pleni, ad litus natabant.

Claudius was the first to jump from the ship into the water, and the other soldiers followed him. The waves were high and cold, but the soldiers, full of courage, swam to the shore.

Cum ad litus pervenissent, vera pugna coepit. Britannos fortes et audaces invenerunt, Romani tamen etiam fortiores erant. Gladiis scutisque, Romani hostes superabant.

When they reached the shore, the real battle began. They found the Britons to be strong and bold, but the Romans were even stronger. With swords and shields, the Romans overcame their enemies.

Post multos labores et proelia, Britannia tandem sub iugum missa est. Claudius, cum commilitonibus suis, in litore stetit, graviter respirans, sed victor.

After many efforts and battles, Britain was finally subdued. Claudius, with his comrades, stood on the shore, breathing heavily, but victorious.

"Hodie," Caesar ad milites dixit, "romana virtus et fortitudo demonstrata est. Claudius, tu omnibus exemplum es!"

"Today," Caesar said to the soldiers, "Roman courage and strength have been demonstrated. Claudius, you are an example to all!"

Et sic, capitulo secundo finito, Claudius et milites Romani primum pedem in Britanniam posuerunt, parati ad novas res gestas et ad gloriae Romanorum augmentum.

And so, with the second chapter finished, Claudius and the Roman soldiers set foot in Britain for the first time, ready for new deeds and to increase the glory of the Romans.

Capitulum Tertium: Prima Proelia

Castra Romana prope litus Britannicum posita sunt. Claudius et ceteri milites, fessi sed animosi, munitiones et vallum firmabant.

The Roman camp was set up near the British shore. Claudius and the other soldiers, weary but spirited, were reinforcing the fortifications and the wall.

"Hodie in terra hostium sumus," Claudius Marcum alloquitur. "Caveamus et fortes simus."

"Today we are in enemy territory," Claudius says to Marcus. "Let us be cautious and strong."

Exploratores in silvas proximas missi sunt, ut motus hostium cognoscerent. Silvae densae et obscurae erant, periculis secretisque plenae.

Scouts were sent into the nearby forests to learn of the enemy's movements. The forests were dense and dark, full of dangers and secrets.

Interim, in castris, nuntius venit: "Hostes in silvis se occultant! Parati ad congressum sumus!"

Meanwhile, in the camp, a messenger arrived: "The enemies are hiding in the forests! We are ready for battle!"

Primum proelium cum Britannis mox coepit. Claudius, in prima acie, gladio suo et scuto bene usus est. In proelio, virtute et audacia conspicuus erat.

The first battle with the Britons soon began. Claudius, in the front line, skillfully used his sword and shield. In the battle, he was distinguished by his bravery and courage.

Multi hostes capti sunt, et Caesar, in castris reversus, Claudium laudavit: "Claudius, tua fortitudo exemplar omnibus est. Roma te honorat!"

Many enemies were captured, and Caesar, upon returning to the camp, praised Claudius: "Claudius, your bravery is an example to all. Rome honors you!"

Nocte in castris, milites de diis Britannis et eorum ritibus fabulabantur. Tumultus et risus inter se miscebantur.

At night in the camp, the soldiers talked about the British gods and their rituals. Noise and laughter mingled among them.

Subito, media nocte, alarma! Hostes castra Romana temptabant. Claudius et milites cito ad arma surrexerunt.

Suddenly, in the middle of the night, an alarm! The enemies were attacking the Roman camp. Claudius and the soldiers quickly rose to arms.

"Ad arma, milites! Hostes appropinquant!" Claudius clamavit. In tenebris, gladii et scuta strepere audiebantur.

"To arms, soldiers! The enemies are approaching!" Claudius shouted. In the darkness, the sounds of swords and shields clashing could be heard.

Hostes repulsi sunt, sed periculum adhuc manebat. Milites, lassitudine oppressi, spolia belli collegerunt et vulneratos curaverunt.

The enemies were repelled, but danger still remained. The soldiers, overcome with exhaustion, gathered the spoils of war and tended to the wounded.

"Fortuna nobiscum est, sed hostes adhuc multos habent," Marcus ad Claudium dixit.

"Fortune is with us, but the enemies still have many men," Marcus said to Claudius.

"Verum est," Claudius respondit. "Sed Romani numquam cedunt. Cras iterum pugnabimus."

"It is true," Claudius replied. "But Romans never surrender. Tomorrow, we will fight again."

Die illo, milites Romanorum virtutem et fortitudinem demonstraverunt. Etiam in terra aliena, sub caelo ignoto, cor Romanum fortiter pulsabat.

On that day, the Roman soldiers demonstrated their courage and strength. Even in foreign land, under an unfamiliar sky, the Roman heart beat strongly.

Consilium de proximo die captum est. Caesar et legati, tabulis et chartis ante se positis, de strategia et consiliis loquebantur.

A plan for the next day was made. Caesar and his lieutenants, with tablets and maps laid before them, discussed strategy and plans.

Claudius, extra tabernaculum Caesaris stans, ad caelum stellatum aspexit et susurravit, "Pro te, Roma, et pro gloria tua, omnia patiar et vincam."

Claudius, standing outside Caesar's tent, looked up at the starry sky and whispered, "For you, Rome, and for your glory, I will endure and conquer all."

Et sic, capitulo tertio finito, Claudius et milites Romani ad novas res gestas et proelia futura parati erant, semper audaces, semper invicti.

And so, with the third chapter finished, Claudius and the Roman soldiers were ready for new deeds and future battles, always brave, always undefeated.

Capitulum Quartum: Silva et Druidae

Claudius, cum manipulo fortium militum, in silvam densam et obscuram missus est. Silva, ramis foliisque condensa, luce solis carebat.

Claudius, with a group of brave soldiers, was sent into a dense and dark forest. The forest, thick with branches and leaves, lacked sunlight.

"Hic locus," Marcus, miles iuxta Claudium, dixit, "mysteriorum plenus est. Druidae, hostes callidi, in hac silva latent."

"This place," said Marcus, a soldier next to Claudius, "is full of mysteries. The Druids, cunning enemies, are hiding in this forest."

Intrinsecus silvae, subito, insidiae Druidarum apparuerunt. Homines barbari ex umbris emerserunt, armati et ad pugnam parati.

Deep within the forest, suddenly, the ambush of the Druids appeared. Barbarian men emerged from the shadows, armed and ready for battle.

"Caveamus!" Claudius exclamavit. "Insidias non timemus!"

"Let us be cautious!" Claudius shouted. "We do not fear ambushes!"

Pugna in silva coepit. Druidae, arcanis artibus et magica utentes, Romanos terrere conabantur. Sed Claudius et milites eius non territi sunt.

The battle in the forest began. The Druids, using mysterious arts and magic, tried to frighten the Romans. But Claudius and his soldiers were not afraid.

"Magica!" unus ex Druidis clamavit, ignesque falsos et imagines terribiles apparuerunt.

"Magic!" one of the Druids shouted, and false fires and terrifying images appeared.

Claudius, gladio suo vibrante, respondit: "Romani magica non timemus! Gladiis nostris pugnamus!"

Claudius, brandishing his sword, responded: "We Romans do not fear magic! We fight with our swords!"

Cum virtute magna, Romani signum suum in medio silvae erexerunt. Druidae, virtute Romana victi, in fugam versi sunt.

With great courage, the Romans raised their standard in the middle of the forest. The Druids, defeated by Roman strength, fled.

Claudius et milites eius castra Druidarum invenerunt, loca secreta et sacra. In castris, signa et instrumenta Druidarum erant, arcanorum plena.

Claudius and his soldiers found the Druids' camp, secret and sacred places. In the camp were the signs and tools of the Druids, full of mystery.

"Videte," Claudius dixit, "haec sunt Druidarum secreta. Nunc artes eorum intellegimus."

"Look," Claudius said, "these are the secrets of the Druids. Now we understand their arts."

Sacra loca Druidarum a Romanis violata sunt. Statuae et altaria eversa sunt, omniaque Druidarum signa capta sunt.

The sacred places of the Druids were violated by the Romans. Statues and altars were overturned, and all the signs of the Druids were captured.

Nuntius ad Caesarem cucurrit, victoriam in silva nuntians. Caesar, audita victoria, laetatus est.

A messenger ran to Caesar, announcing victory in the forest. Caesar, hearing of the victory, was delighted.

"Claudius et milites eius fortitudinem et audaciam demonstraverunt," Caesar dixit. "Hodie, Roma in silvis Britanniae victoriam habet."

"Claudius and his soldiers have shown courage and bravery," Caesar said. "Today, Rome has victory in the forests of Britain."

Claudius, ad castra reversus, laudem a Caesare et commilitonibus accepit. Eius virtus et audacia in omnibus manifestae erant.

Claudius, upon returning to the camp, received praise from Caesar and his comrades. His courage and bravery were clear to all.

Nocte, cum omnes in castris dormirent, silva adhuc mysteria sua habebat. Venti per arbores sibilabant, lumenque lunae inter folia lucebat.

At night, while everyone in the camp slept, the forest still held its mysteries. The winds whispered through the trees, and the moonlight shone between the leaves.

Claudius, sub astris dormiens, de futuris pugnis et gloria Romae somniabat. Et sic, capitulo quarto finito, Claudius et milites Romani ad novas res gestas parati erant, semper fortes, semper invicti.

Claudius, sleeping under the stars, dreamed of future battles and the glory of Rome. And so, with the fourth chapter finished, Claudius and the Roman soldiers were ready for new deeds, always strong, always undefeated.

Capitulum Quintum: Britannia Profunda

Caesar, dux Romanorum, explorare profundam Britanniam iussit. Claudius, fortis miles, cum exploratoribus iter incepit.

Caesar, the leader of the Romans, ordered an exploration of the depths of Britain. Claudius, a brave soldier, began the journey with the scouts.

"In hac terra," Claudius Marcum alloquitur, "flumina et montes nobis obstacula sunt. Sed Romani semper progrediuntur!"

"In this land," Claudius said to Marcus, "rivers and mountains are obstacles for us. But Romans always advance!"

Tranquille flumina transierunt et altos montes superaverunt. Subito, villae Britannorum in conspectu erant, fumo ex focis surgente.

They crossed the rivers calmly and climbed the high mountains. Suddenly, the villages of the Britons were in sight, with smoke rising from the hearths.

"Videte," Claudius dixit, "Britanni hic vivunt. Pacem cum eis faciemus."

"Look," Claudius said, "The Britons live here. We will make peace with them."

Legati Romani ad villam accesserunt, pacem cum quibusdam tribubus Britannorum facientes. Sed non omnes Britanni pacem volebant.

Roman envoys approached the village, making peace with some of the British tribes. But not all Britons wanted peace.

Alii Britanni, bellicoso animo, ad bellum contra Romanos surrexerunt. Pugnae difficiles in apertis campis coeperunt.

Other Britons, with a warlike spirit, rose up to fight against the Romans. Difficult battles began in the open fields.

Claudius, in medio proelii, fortiter pugnabat. Sed, in tumultu, vulneratus est. Gladius hostis eius brachium percussit.

Claudius, in the middle of the battle, fought bravely. But in the chaos, he was wounded. The enemy's sword struck his arm.

"Claudius vulneratus est!" Marcus exclamavit. Medicus statim ad eum cucurrit, vulnera eius curans.

"Claudius is wounded!" Marcus exclaimed. A medic quickly ran to him, tending to his wounds.

Milites Romani, in terra hostili fatigati, tamen pugnabant. Interim, rebellio in Britannia crescebat, hostesque Romanos undique circumdabant.

The Roman soldiers, tired in hostile territory, still fought on. Meanwhile, the rebellion in Britain was growing, and enemies surrounded the Romans from all sides.

Caesar, audita difficultate, novas copias ad Britanniam misit. Auxilium Romanorum venit.

Caesar, upon hearing of the difficulty, sent new troops to Britain. Roman reinforcements arrived.

Claudius, convalescens, rursus ad pugnas rediit. "Non cessabo," inquit, "dum Roma me vocat!"

Claudius, recovering, returned to the battles once more. "I will not stop," he said, "while Rome calls me!"

Nocte quadam, Claudius et milites eius hostium castra adoriri statuerunt. Sub luna, silentio, ad castra hostium accesserunt.

One night, Claudius and his soldiers decided to attack the enemy camp. Under the moon, in silence, they approached the enemy camp.

"Nunc," Claudius susurravit, "Romanorum virtus ostendetur!"

"Now," Claudius whispered, "The bravery of the Romans will be shown!"

Romani, repente, in hostium castra irruperunt. Pugna acris erat, sed Romani praevaluerunt. Hostes in fugam versi sunt.

The Romans suddenly stormed into the enemy camp. The battle was fierce, but the Romans prevailed. The enemies fled.

Post proelium, nuntius ad Caesarem cucurrit, magnam victoriam nuntians. "Claudius et milites eius hostes vicerunt!" exclamavit.

After the battle, a messenger ran to Caesar, announcing a great victory. "Claudius and his soldiers have defeated the enemies!" he exclaimed.

Caesar, audita victoria, laetatus est. "Claudius," inquit, "dux fortis et fidelis es. Grati sumus pro tua virtute!"

Caesar, upon hearing of the victory, was pleased. "Claudius," he said, "you are a brave and loyal leader. We are grateful for your courage!"

Claudius, in castris Romanis, inter commilitones suos stetit, vultu sereno. "Pro Roma, pro gloria, semper pugnabimus," inquit.

Claudius, standing among his comrades in the Roman camp, with a calm expression, said, "For Rome, for glory, we will always fight."

Et sic, capitulo quinto finito, Claudius et milites Romani ad novas res gestas parati erant, semper audaces, semper invicti, semper pro gloria Romae pugnantes.

And so, with the fifth chapter finished, Claudius and the Roman soldiers were ready for new deeds, always brave, always undefeated, always fighting for the glory of Rome.

Capitulum Sextum: Mare et Monstra

Caesar, rebus gestis in Britannia finitis, reditum ad litus iussit. Claudius, miles audax, navem ducere coepit.

Caesar, after finishing his deeds in Britain, ordered a return to the shore. Claudius, the bold soldier, began to lead the ship.

"Hoc mare," Claudius Marcum alloquitur, "multa monstra habere dicitur. Fabulae nautarum sunt plenae terribilibus bestiis."

"This sea," Claudius said to Marcus, "is said to have many monsters. Sailors' tales are full of terrible beasts."

Marcus ridet, "Haec fabulae sunt, Claudius! Monstra maris non vere existunt."

Marcus laughed, "These are just stories, Claudius! Sea monsters don't really exist."

Sed iter non facile erat. Subito, magna tempestas oritur, ventis magnis et undis altis. Navigatio difficilis facta est.

But the journey was not easy. Suddenly, a great storm arose, with strong winds and high waves. Sailing became difficult.

Claudius, in prora navis stans, nautis animos addit. "Ne timeatis!" inquit. "Romani etiam in mari fortes sumus!"

Claudius, standing at the bow of the ship, encouraged the sailors. "Do not fear!" he said. "We Romans are strong, even at sea!"

Dum tempestas furit, cetus magnus, bestia marina ingens, navem sequitur. Milites et nautae, bestiam videntes, maximo pavore affecti sunt.

While the storm raged, a great whale, a huge sea creature, followed the ship. The soldiers and sailors, seeing the beast, were struck with great fear.

"Cetus!" unus ex militibus clamavit. "Monstrum maris vere est!"

"A whale!" one of the soldiers shouted. "It really is a sea monster!"

Sed Claudius, fortitudinem suam servans, milites et nautas adhortatus est, "Ne timemus! In hoc mari, Romani etiam fortiores sumus!"

But Claudius, maintaining his courage, encouraged the soldiers and sailors, "Let us not fear! In this sea, we Romans are even stronger!"

Miraculo, cetus tandem discessit, et sol iterum in caelo apparet. Milites et nautae, solati, ad navigandum se paraverunt.

Miraculously, the whale finally left, and the sun appeared again in the sky. The soldiers and sailors, relieved, prepared to sail once more.

Claudius, looking back at the British shore, said, "Farewell, Britain! Perhaps we will see you again."

The ships, with favorable winds, were headed towards Gaul. But the dangers of the sea still remained. Some ships, devastated by the storm, were lost.

Claudius, on his ship, thought about the dangers of the sea and the strength of the Romans. "This sea," he said, "tests us, but Romans always prevail."

After a day and night, they finally saw the Gallic shore. Claudius and his soldiers, seeing land, were filled with joy.

"Gaul!" Marcus exclaimed. "Our land! How beautiful it is!"

The ships approached the shore, and the soldiers, feeling solid ground, disembarked. Claudius, standing on the shore, looked back at the sea.

"The sea and monsters," he said, "tested us, but we Romans are strong and undefeated."

Et sic, capitulo sexto finito, Claudius et milites Romani, rebus gestis novis et periculis superatis, parati erant, semper audaces, semper fortes, semper pro gloria et honore Romae pugnantes.

And so, with the sixth chapter finished, Claudius and the Roman soldiers, having faced new challenges and overcome dangers, were ready, always brave, always strong, always fighting for the glory and honor of Rome.

Capitulum Septimum: Ultima Proelia

Postquam Britannia relicta est, Gallia petita est. Caesar, dux Romanorum, ultima proelia contra Gallos parabat. Claudius, in castris Romanis, fiduciam in Caesaris ducatum habebat.

After Britain was left behind, Gaul was the next target. Caesar, the leader of the Romans, was preparing for the final battles against the Gauls. Claudius, in the Roman camp, had confidence in Caesar's leadership.

"Hodie," Claudius Marcum alloquitur, "ultima proelia nobis sunt. Hostes in silvis latent, sed eos inveniemus et vincemus."

"Today," Claudius said to Marcus, "these are our final battles. The enemies are hiding in the forests, but we will find them and defeat them."

Milites Romani in silvas densas intraverunt, hostes Gallicos quaerentes. In silvis, pugnae durissimae fiebant.

The Roman soldiers entered the dense forests, searching for the Gallic enemies. In the forests, very fierce battles were taking place.

Claudius, dux fortis et peritus, in proeliis clarus efficitur. Cum gladio suo et scuto, in prima acie pugnabat.

Claudius, a strong and skilled leader, became renowned in the battles. With his sword and shield, he fought in the front line.

Multae victoriae a Romanis reportabantur. Claudius, in omnibus proeliis, virtutem et audaciam ostendebat.

Many victories were won by the Romans. Claudius, in all the battles, showed bravery and courage.

Subito, nuntius ad castra venit: "Rebellio aliarum tribuum Gallicarum!" Nuntius exclamavit. "Caesar ad novum bellum movet!"

Suddenly, a messenger arrived at the camp: "Rebellion of other Gallic tribes!" the messenger exclaimed. "Caesar is moving towards a new war!"

Caesar, audito nuntio, milites ad bellum novum paravit. "Claudius," Caesar dixit, "tu signifer eris. In te et in tua virtute confido."

Caesar, upon hearing the message, prepared the soldiers for a new war. "Claudius," Caesar said, "you will be the standard-bearer. I trust in you and your courage."

Claudius, signo Romano in manu, dux magnus factus est. Nova castra, prope hostium terras, fiunt.

Claudius, with the Roman standard in hand, became a great leader. New camps were built near the enemy lands.

"In his proeliis," Claudius militibus dixit, "fortitudo et fides nostra probabuntur."

"In these battles," Claudius said to the soldiers, "our strength and loyalty will be tested."

Insidiae hostium, arte et prudentia Romanorum, evitatae sunt. Romani, in hostes impetum facientes, eos superabant.

The enemy's traps were avoided by the skill and wisdom of the Romans. The Romans, attacking the enemies, overcame them.

Ultimum bellum contra Gallos coeptum est. Pugna magna et acris erat, sed Romani, sub duce Caesare et signifero Claudio, praevaluerunt.

The final war against the Gauls began. The battle was great and fierce, but the Romans, under the leadership of Caesar and standard-bearer Claudius, prevailed.

Post proelium, victoria Caesaris clara erat. Galli, virtute Romanorum victi, pacem petebant.

After the battle, Caesar's victory was clear. The Gauls, defeated by the strength of the Romans, sought peace.

Caesar, in castris Romanis, Claudium ad se vocavit. "Claudius," Caesar inquit, "pro meritis tuis, gloriam et honores accipies. Roma te laudat!"

Caesar, in the Roman camp, called Claudius to him. "Claudius," Caesar said, "for your merits, you will receive glory and honors. Rome praises you!"

Claudius, coram militibus et Caesare, honores accepit. "Pro Roma," inquit Claudius, "omnia pati et vincere paratus sum."

Claudius, in the presence of the soldiers and Caesar, received honors. "For Rome," Claudius said, "I am ready to endure and conquer all."

Et sic, capitulo septimo finito, Claudius et milites Romani, novis victoriis et gloriam accipientes, parati erant, semper fortes, semper audaces, semper pro gloria et honore Romae pugnantes.

And so, with the seventh chapter finished, Claudius and the Roman soldiers, receiving new victories and glory, were ready, always strong, always brave, always fighting for the glory and honor of Rome.

Capitulum Octavum: Reditus in Galliam

Claudius, cum Caesare et militibus, in Galliam redit. Triumphus magnus Romae paratur, victorias in Britannia et Gallia celebraturus.

Claudius, with Caesar and the soldiers, returned to Gaul. A great triumph was being prepared in Rome to celebrate the victories in Britain and Gaul.

Claudius, iter faciens, de futuris rebus cogitat. "Quae mihi in vita futura sunt?" se ipse interrogat.

Claudius, making his journey, thought about future things. "What lies ahead for me in life?" he asked himself.

Ad castra Romana appropinquans, amicos et familiam suam videt. Gaudio magno excipiuntur.

Approaching the Roman camp, he saw his friends and family. They were received with great joy.

Caesar, in medio militum, Claudium laudat. "Claudius," inquit, "miles fortis et fidelis, multas victorias nobis attulisti."

Caesar, in the midst of the soldiers, praised Claudius. "Claudius," he said, "brave and loyal soldier, you have brought us many victories."

Sub Caesare, Galli pacati sunt. Claudius, pro meritis suis, agrum in terra sua accipit.

Under Caesar, the Gauls were pacified. Claudius, for his merits, received land in his own country.

Nuntii de novis imperiis et expeditionibus ad Claudium veniunt. "Semper ad novas res gestas paratus sum," dicit Claudius.

News of new empires and expeditions came to Claudius. "I am always ready for new deeds," said Claudius.

Pax in Gallia celebratur. Ludi et festivitates fiunt, victoriam Romanorum laudantes.

Peace was celebrated in Gaul. Games and festivals were held, praising the Roman victory.

Veterani milites, inter quos Claudius, honores accipiunt. Coronae, diplomata, et dona a Caesare eis dantur.

Veteran soldiers, among them Claudius, received honors. Crowns, diplomas, and gifts were given to them by Caesar.

Sacrificia deis Romanis fiunt. Sacerdotes preces et hostias deis offerunt, pro salute et fortuna Imperii Romani.

Sacrifices were made to the Roman gods. Priests offered prayers and sacrifices to the gods for the safety and fortune of the Roman Empire.

Claudius, quiete momento fruens, de vita militari et pace cogitat. "Vita militaris dura est, sed pax et securitas pro Roma nobis cara sunt," meditatur.

Claudius, enjoying a moment of peace, thought about military life and peace. "Military life is hard, but peace and security for Rome are dear to us," he pondered.

Epistulae ad familias Romanas mittuntur, victorias et reditum militum nuntiantes. Familiae, epistulas legentes, laetantur et gratias agunt.

Letters were sent to Roman families, announcing the victories and the return of the soldiers. Families, reading the letters, rejoiced and gave thanks.

Claudius, tandem, novam vitam inchoat. Terra sua, amicis et familia circumdatus, novas res et futurum suum contemplat.

Claudius, at last, began a new life. Surrounded by his land, friends, and family, he contemplated new things and his future.

"Roma me vocavit," dicit Claudius, "et pro ea pugnavi. Nunc nova vita me exspectat."

"Rome called me," Claudius said, "and I fought for her. Now a new life awaits me."

Et sic, capitulo octavo finito, Claudius et milites Romani, ad novam vitam in Imperio Romano parati, semper fortes, semper audaces, semper Romae fideles erant.

And so, with the eighth chapter finished, Claudius and the Roman soldiers, prepared for a new life in the Roman Empire, were always strong, always brave, and always loyal to Rome.

De Caesaris Factis in Britannia

Julius Caesar, Romanorum dux magnus, Britanniam bis invasit. Hae expeditiones magnae in annis quinquagesimo quinto et quinquagesimo quarto ante Christum natum factae sunt.

Julius Caesar, the great leader of the Romans, invaded Britain twice. These great expeditions took place in 55 and 54 B.C.

Prima Expeditio:

• *Caesar, cum Romanis militibus, in Britanniam navigavit.*

The First Expedition: • Caesar, with Roman soldiers, sailed to Britain.

• *In litore Britannico pugnavit.*

• He fought on the British shore.

• *Britanni, fortiter resistebant.*

• The Britons resisted bravely.

• *Romanorum copiae, tempestatibus affectae, difficultates habuerunt.*

• The Roman forces, affected by storms, encountered difficulties.

• *Caesar in Galliam rediit, sed Britanniam iterum invadere statuit.*

• Caesar returned to Gaul, but decided to invade Britain again.

Secunda Expeditio:

• *Caesar cum pluribus militibus rediit.*

The Second Expedition: • Caesar returned with more soldiers.

• *Multas pugnas contra Britannos fecit.*

• He fought many battles against the Britons.

• *Britanniae civitates, a Caesare victae, obsides dederunt.*

• The British states, defeated by Caesar, gave hostages.

• *Caesar, Britannos superatis, gloriam magnam Romae rettulit.*

• Caesar, after defeating the Britons, brought great glory to Rome.

• *Pax inter Romanos et Britannos facta est.*

• Peace was made between the Romans and Britons.

Haec Caesaris facta in Britannia Romae laudem et gloriam attulerunt. Caesar, dux audax et peritus, Romanorum imperium ampliavit.

These deeds of Caesar in Britain brought praise and glory to Rome. Caesar, a bold and skilled leader, expanded the Roman Empire.

More books

More ressources

Endorsements by leading Latinists

All on discoverlatin.com